Guidebook on the

Law and Practice of

Soil and Water
Conservation

in North Carolina

Edited by Milton S. Heath, Jr.

2004

I0109618

UNC
SCHOOL OF GOVERNMENT

THE UNIVERSITY
of NORTH CAROLINA
at CHAPEL HILL

School of Government | UNC Chapel Hill

Established in 1931, the Institute of Government provides training, advisory, and research services to public officials and others interested in the operation of state and local government in North Carolina. The Institute and the university's Master of Public Administration Program are the core activities of the School of Government at The University of North Carolina at Chapel Hill.

Each year approximately 14,000 public officials and others attend one or more of the more than 200 classes, seminars, and conferences offered by the Institute. Faculty members annually publish up to fifty books, bulletins, and other reference works related to state and local government. Each day that the General Assembly is in session, the Institute's *Daily Bulletin*, available in print and electronic format, reports on the day's activities for members of the legislature and others who need to follow the course of legislation. An extensive Web site (www.sog.unc.edu) provides access to publications and faculty research, course listings, program and service information, and links to other useful sites related to government.

Operating support for the School of Government's programs and activities comes from many sources, including state appropriations, local government membership dues, private contributions, publication sales, course fees, and service contracts. For more information about the School, the Institute, and the MPA program, visit the Web site or call (919) 966-5381.

Michael R. Smith, DEAN
Patricia A. Langelier, ASSOCIATE DEAN FOR OPERATIONS
Ann Cary Simpson, ASSOCIATE DEAN FOR DEVELOPMENT AND COMMUNICATIONS
Thomas H. Thornburg, SENIOR ASSOCIATE DEAN FOR PROGRAMS
Ted D. Zoller, ASSOCIATE DEAN FOR BUSINESS AND FINANCE

FACULTY

Gregory S. Allison
Stephen Allred (on leave)
David N. Ammons
A. Fleming Bell, II
Frayda S. Bluestein
Mark F. Botts
Phillip Boyle
Joan G. Brannon
Mary Maureen Brown
Anita R. Brown-Graham
William A. Campbell
Anne M. Dellinger
Shea Riggsbee Denning
James C. Drennan

Richard D. Ducker
Robert L. Farb
Joseph S. Ferrell
Milton S. Heath, Jr.
Cheryl Daniels Howell
Joseph E. Hunt
Willow Jacobson
Robert P. Joyce
Diane Juffras
David M. Lawrence
Janet Mason
Laurie L. Mesibov
Jill D. Moore
Jonathan Morgan

David W. Owens
William C. Rivenbark
John Rubin
John L. Saxon
Jessica Smith
Carl Stenberg
John B. Stephens
Vaughn Upshaw
A. John Vogt
Aimee Wall
Mark Weidemaier
Richard Whisnant
Gordon P. Whitaker

Contents

              Partnership   133
              Dick Fowler

Indexes   137

              Case Index   139

              Subject Index   141

              Proper Name Index   145

Foreword

In the 1930s and 1940s, when soil and water conservation districts were first formed in North Carolina, healing deep gullies and restoring "worn out" farms to agricultural production was the backbone of most local conservation programs. Tree planting, brush gully plugs, and contour terraces joined grass and other plantings to control erosion in farm fields. Predominantly, conservation district leadership in the early days was made up of farmers helping other farmers, with support from the United States Department of Agriculture.

Today, conservation districts' programs are much more complex, dealing with urban as well as agricultural issues and involving many players. Environmental issues, such as water quality and non-point source pollution, consume a major portion of districts' time and attention. Support for districts' conservation programs comes from federal, state, and local government sources and from the private sector. Conservation district leadership comes from many sectors of the communities served and includes people with special interests that go well beyond traditions of supervisors in the early days of the conservation movement.

It was the need to have broad conservation programs that respond to today's issues and district boards of supervisors who are prepared to lead the conservation effort in their communities that fostered this *Guidebook on the Law and Practice of Soil and Water Conservation in North Carolina*. The *Guidebook* was written as a collaborative effort of several people, with Milton Heath of the University of North Carolina's Institute of Government serving as coordinator and primary author. It contains key information and guidance needed by district supervisors and support staff for conducting a conservation program that is responsive and that leads to meeting the needs of people and the natural environment in our state.

In this *Guidebook* you will find an accounting of various laws, rules, and regulations that guide and control the actions of district supervisors and staff in shaping the conservation program and operation of your conservation district. You will also find information on the collection of governmental agencies and programs available to support the creation and conduct of a comprehensive conservation program in your district.

The North Carolina Foundation for Soil & Water Conservation Districts is pleased to have a part in creating this *Guidebook*. It puts into a single place, as a ready reference, basic information and guidance needed to help you succeed in leading and guiding the conservation effort in your community. It also helps the Foundation address one of its three major goals—building capacity in conservation districts.

Financial support from Altria Group, Inc., and Progress Energy turned this project into reality. The North Carolina Conservation Partnership added support by endorsing the idea for the *Guidebook*. We thank all contributors for your financial support or expertise given to this project helping to build capacity in conservation districts throughout North Carolina. Now we encourage district supervisors to take full advantage of this resource as you lead your districts.

Cecil Settle
Executive Director
North Carolina Foundation for
Soil & Water Conservation Districts

Preface

This *Guidebook* is a work in progress that is a product of twenty years of basic schools held by the Institute of Government to train supervisors of soil and water conservation districts in North Carolina. Ten of its fourteen chapters have their origins in the "schoolbooks" used in the basic schools and in training exercises conducted at area meetings of the state Association of Soil and Water Conservation Districts. I am the principal author of those ten chapters. Senior soil and water conservation leaders, to whom the Institute owes a special debt of gratitude, authored the remaining chapters:

Chapter 1, "History of Soil and Water Conservation Districts in North Carolina," Charles Bullock (former head of district operations, N.C. Division of Soil and Water Conservation) and Dr. Maurice Cook (professor emeritus of soil sciences, North Carolina State University)

Chapter 10, "The North Carolina Conservation District Employees' Association," Gail M. Hughes (Orange County District soil conservationist and former president of the District Employees' Association)

Chapter 13, "Federal Programs of Interest to Districts," Dick Fowler (assistant state conservationist, Natural Resources Conservation Service, North Carolina)

Chapter 14, "Three Basic Agreements That Support the Conservation Partnership," Dick Fowler

Valuable contributions were made to Chapter 2, "Organization and Administration of Programs," by Lynn Sprague, head of district operations of the N.C. Division of Soil and Water Conservation and by Cecil Settle. David Vogel, director of the N.C. Division of Soil and Water Conservation, helped author parts of Chapter 5, "Powers and Duties of Soil and Water Conservation Supervisors and Districts."

Dick Fowler of the Natural Resources Conservation Service (NRCS) provided indefatigable peer review of a number of chapters, as did Cecil Settle, Lynn Sprague, and Jerry Dorsett (area coordinator for Area 3). My Institute colleagues David Lawrence and Jack Vogt and Deputy Attorney General Ryke Longest supplied peer review of the chapters on "Laws That Impose Legal Duties or Restrictions on a District," "District Finance," and "Liability Issues." School of Government Senior Associate Dean Tom Thornburg kept a steady hand on the forward progress of this project, and Publications Director Angela Williams kept the publication moving. Lucille Fidler, also of the School of Government, and Marion Laird supplied valuable editorial review. Daniel Soileau provided design services.

The Institute and I are especially indebted to Cecil Settle, the executive director of the North Carolina Foundation for Soil & Water Conservation Districts, not only for his contributions to the book itself, but for his essential efforts in obtaining the financial support required for this project. The financial support that he secured from Altria Group, Inc., and Progress Energy, as he put it, "turned this project into reality." The Institute and I are truly grateful to them and to the Foundation for backing this project from its inception.

For two decades we have held Institute soil and water conservation schools with an informal schoolbook as source material. The time has now come to move forward into future training programs with this finished *Guidebook* in hand.

Milton S. Heath, Jr., Editor
Professor of Public Law and Government
Institute of Government
School of Government
University of North Carolina at Chapel Hill
August 2004

1

History of Soil and Water Conservation Districts in North Carolina

Charles Bullock and Dr. Maurice Cook

Why is the history of soil and water conservation districts worth recording and remembering? Organizations, like people, need a sense of their "roots" to understand and appreciate their character. This, in turn, enables people and organizations to better understand their reason for being and to move confidently into the future.

Harry Truman was once quoted as saying that the only thing new in the world is the history we have forgotten. The historical record tends to bear that out. District supervisors, strengthened with a knowledge of their history, can apply lessons learned in the past to current and future issues.

Soil and water conservation districts in North Carolina have an exciting and memorable history. It would be impossible to describe in a single chapter the far-reaching impact of districts. Interaction with other agencies and their implementation of conservation programs has been too extensive to adequately address here. The aim of this writing is to simply present a chronological documentation of the establishment, growth, and development of soil and water conservation districts in North Carolina, with the hope that their rich and noble history will inspire all who work with districts to reach even greater heights in the future.

Charles Bullock is the former head of district operations for the N.C. Division of Soil and Water Conservation. Dr. Maurice Cook is professor emeritus of soil sciences at North Carolina State University.

Need for Districts

The conservation district idea emerged in the mid-1930s. It was conceived as a way of bridging the gap between federal technicians and private landowners. Many people were involved in the generation of the idea and the creation of the mechanism to make districts a reality. One person, however, stands above the others as the leader who made it happen. He was Dr. Hugh Hammond Bennett, one of North Carolina's most prominent citizens. Bennett was known as the "Father of Soil Conservation" and rightly so. He was the driving force behind the soil conservation movement that has had such a dramatic, positive effect on the landscape of America. The soil conservation story cannot be told without first paying tribute to Bennett, who brought the issue of soil erosion to the nation's attention. His strong leadership resulted in a national soil conservation program of tremendous dimensions.

Bennett's concern for the land and the mammoth losses of soil as a result of soil erosion dated back to 1905, when he and his soil survey partner, W. E. McLendon, developed a theory of sheet erosion—the insidious but largely unseen washing away of thin layers of topsoil. From then on, Bennett never stopped talking and writing about what was happening to the land in America. But it was 1930 before he gained public support for his cause. It was primarily Bennett's persistence and persuasiveness that finally led to a $160,000 federal appropriation in 1930 for soil erosion investigations.

These funds were used to establish ten erosion stations. Bennett had a large hand in the establishment and work of these stations. He selected most of the sites and outlined most of the studies. A vast amount of information was acquired and made public. More than 300,000 quantitative measurements were made of soil and water losses under differing conditions of land use, management, treatment, and cover. The results of these studies, supported by increasing agricultural appropriations, led to the establishment of the Soil Erosion Service in the Department of the Interior in September 1933. Hugh Hammond Bennett was appointed the agency's first director. In eighteen months, forty-one soil and water conservation demonstration projects were established and about fifty civilian conservation corps camps were assigned to the work.

Dr. Hugh Hammond Bennett

Dr. Hugh Hammond Bennett, left.

Photos courtesy of USDA Natural Resources Conservation Service.

The success of Bennett's demonstration projects, aided by the disastrous Dust Bowl of the 1930s, brought a large public outcry for a national policy on soil erosion control. Action was swift. U.S. Public Law 46, the Soil Conservation Act, was passed in 1935. The act created the Soil Conservation Service (SCS), and it also established a national policy, namely, "To provide for the protection of land resources against soil erosion, and other purposes." It is doubtful that a national soil conservation policy and a federal soil conservation agency would have been created so rapidly and so dramatically without Bennett's vision and vigorous leadership.

The demonstration program showed that erosion control measures developed through research were practical and could be applied on land if the necessary information and technical assistance could be provided. It was increasingly evident that farmers and landowners needed to participate much more in the planning and implementation of conservation practices. Thus, the conservation districts idea began to evolve.

Although Dr. Bennett worked for a federal agency, he was keenly aware of the need for state and local involvement in the conservation movement. In fact, many believe that the concept of local districts was one of Bennett's greatest achievements.

The Beginning

The first step was to develop a proposal for state legislation that could put the idea into action. The result was the development of a model act for use as a guide by state legislatures. This model legislation, called the Standard State District Act and known as the Standard Act or District Law, provided that land occupiers could organize soil conservation districts as local governmental subdivisions of the state. It set up procedures for establishing districts and defined their duties and powers.

In 1937 President Roosevelt sent a letter to the nation's governors urging them to adopt the Standard State District law. Each state responded and passed such legislation. Although not the first state to adopt the District Law, North Carolina was the first state to organize a conservation district. Appropriately enough, the first district was the Brown Creek Soil Conservation District, organized on August 4, 1937. It encompassed the Brown Creek watershed, the site of Bennett's home in Anson County.

That same year the North Carolina General Assembly passed Chapter 139 of the North Carolina General Statutes (hereinafter G.S.), which contained several historic measures. G.S. 139-4 created a soil conservation agency known as the State Soil Conservation Committee or State Committee. This committee was composed of three people: the director of the Agricultural Extension Service, the director of the Agricultural Experiment Stations, and the state forester. All of these were housed at North Carolina State College (now North Carolina State University).

G.S. 139-5 established the framework for creation of soil conservation districts, under the supervision of the State Committee. Each district was organized through the efforts of local citizens and managed by a local board of supervisors. A petition containing the names of twenty-five local occupiers of land led to a land-occupier referendum and final approval by the State Committee.

G.S. 139-6 provided for the election of three members of each district board of supervisors. These elections took place at country stores and other gathering places where farmers congregated. They were called "shoe box elections" by many. In 1973 legislation moved the election of these district supervisors to the general election. As a result, beginning in 1974, district board members were elected at the same time as other county officials. This raised the visibility of districts and gave the elections more credibility.

G.S. 139-7 provided for the appointment of members—two for each district—to the local board by the State Committee. This enabled local boards to enlist the help of people who might not have sought the job but who had expertise the district needed. No distinction was made between the voting powers or legal status of the elected and the appointed members of the board.

G.S. 139-7 also gave the local boards of supervisors authority "to employ a secretary, technical experts, and such other employees as they may require, and shall determine their qualifications, duties, and compensation." And it gave them the authority to "call upon the Attorney General of the State for such legal services as they may require."

G.S. 139-8 established soil conservation districts as governmental subdivisions of the state of North Carolina and spelled out the general powers of districts and the boards of supervisors.

In 1944 the districts organized a State Association of Conservation Districts. O. J. Holler, a district supervisor from Union Mills, was

elected the first president. The stage was now set for the participation
of federal, state, and local agencies in a statewide conservation effort.
This was another step toward realizing Bennett's vision for soil
conservation.

Organizational Growth and Development

The Standard Act did not provide guidelines for establishing district
boundaries. At first, districts followed watershed boundaries, which
meant that most of the districts included more than one county or
parts of several counties. USDA leaders generally favored watershed
boundaries for districts while most of the state laws were based on
county boundaries.

The first districts were all multi-county districts. By 1955 all 100
counties had held elections and each county was a part of a conservation district. Districts began to reorganize along county lines in the
early 1960s, thus breaking up the multi-county units. As of the year
2004, there is only one multi-county district in the entire state, the
Albemarle District, consisting of Camden, Chowan, Currituck,
Pasquotank, and Perquimans counties.

As the district movement grew and more local citizens became
involved, there was a need to expand the membership of the original
State Committee. This was done in 1947 when the president, vice pres-
ident and immediate past president of the Association of Conservation
Districts were added as members. James Bellamy from the Brunswick
District was the first supervisor to serve as chairman of the State
Committee.

In 1959 the General Assembly appropriated funds to hire an
administrative officer for the State Committee. Bryce Younts was
hired, and he thus became the first salaried employee. The 1959
General Assembly also amended the District Law to enable districts
and counties to sponsor small watershed (or "watershed improvement") projects. Congress had already authorized federal support for
small watershed projects in Public Law 566, and this stimulated interest in the districts.

In 1961 the name of the committee was changed to the North
Carolina Soil and Water Conservation Committee, and the SCS state
conservationist was added to the committee as a non-voting member.

Likewise, the state association name was changed to the North Carolina Association of Soil and Water Conservation Districts. This marked a new emphasis on water conservation, reflected in the 1959 Small Watershed Amendments, that was to become a major theme for the future.

The state agency continued to grow. In 1965 the General Assembly appropriated funds to hire an assistant administrative officer. Before the new position could be filled, though, Bryce Younts resigned and Jack Smith was hired to replace him. These two individuals played a very important role in shaping both the state agency and the local districts.

Chapter 139 of the General Statutes was revised in 1971 to allow the North Carolina Association of Soil and Water Conservation Districts to elect three members to the North Carolina (or "State") Soil and Water Conservation Committee, one for each major geographical region of the state. The committee was permitted to appoint one member at-large. This brought membership of the committee to seven.

The overall reorganization of state government from 1973 to 1975 had an enormous impact on the state conservation agency. The administrative officer and staff were moved into the Division of Earth Resources in the Department of Natural and Economic Resources. As a result of that move, the name of the Soil and Water Conservation Committee was changed to the North Carolina Soil and Water Conservation Commission (the State Commission). Provision was also made for the Governor to appoint the seventh member, who would serve as chairman of the commission.

In 1977 the Department of Natural and Economic Resources was reorganized again, and its name changed to the Department of Natural Resources and Community Development. The Division of Earth Resources became the Division of Land Resources. It continued to be the home of the State Commission.

In 1979 the Division of Soil and Water Conservation was established in the Department of Natural Resources and Community Development. Dr. Joseph A. Phillips, a professor of soil science at North Carolina State University, was named the first director. The State Commission was shifted from the Division of Land Resources to this new division. In 1981 the commission assumed responsibility for supervising water improvement districts.

New and Expanded Program Responsibilities

The establishment of the Division of Soil and Water Conservation as an integral component of a state agency brought additional roles and responsibilities for districts. The 1970s saw a marked increase in national concern for environmental issues such as water quality. Amendments to the U.S. Clean Water Act addressed non-point source pollution, which brought agriculture and forestry into the clean water debate for the first time. As a result, a new section was added to the division, the Nonpoint Source Pollution Control Section. This, in turn, led to the formation of the Agricultural Task Force, a consortium of agricultural agencies and organizations, to evaluate the role of agriculture in non-point source pollution and to recommend action to reduce it. These actions at the state level had significant implications for districts as they assumed a greater role in water quality assessments and programs at the local level.

Another new section, Soil Survey, was added to the division to assist SCS with a cooperative soil survey program in the state. Districts assumed a significant role in those counties requiring new or revised soil surveys.

An existing section, Watershed Improvement, assumed more responsibility in watershed activities. This affected a large number of districts that have concerns about agricultural flooding, wetlands, drainage, and overall management. Various reorganizations have produced the current sections as of the year 2004—district operations, technical services, non-point source programs, and administrative services.

These three sections work closely with the area coordinators, who were added in the 1990s, to develop and implement programs for local districts. In general, districts have accepted well the new roles and responsibilities given them, which is a tribute to the districts' flexibility and creativity in solving problems and meeting new challenges.

Federal-State-Local Relationships

During the first three decades of their existence, districts were dependent on the federal agency, SCS, for most of their funding, administration, and technical support. (SCS was renamed the Natural Resource Conservation Service or NRCS in the 1990s.) However, during the past three decades, state and local agencies have assumed a much greater role in personnel and program support. In the late 1980s and throughout the 1990s, districts or counties hired administrative and technical personnel to supplement the federal source. County governments have provided increasing support for local soil and water conservation. This process has accelerated to the point that the total number of local employees in local offices in the state now exceeds the number of federal employees. The large body of local employees led to the establishment of the District Employees Association, which is now an influential voice in the soil and water conservation dialogue within North Carolina.

Some have likened the soil and water conservation movement to a three-legged stool with strong federal, state, and local support. That seems to be an appropriate analogy. North Carolina has one of the best conservation teams in America and that has happened because of the efforts of many people. Only a few names have been mentioned here. Countless unnamed people at the federal, state, and local levels have devoted their lives to the movement that Dr. Bennett initiated.

Epilogue

The record of soil and water conservation districts is superb. The words of Hugh Hammond Bennett should continually encourage and inspire us: "I consider the soil conservation district movement one of the most important developments in the whole history of agriculture. It has proved more effective, I am convinced, than we had dared to expect."

How will districts change to meet the challenges of the twenty-first century? Obviously, no one can predict what the future holds for districts. We do know that their future will start with what they have and where they are today. As we have observed in the latter part of the twentieth century, many of the issues that were considered "new" then were likely to have been considered "new" in 1935, 1965, or some other time in the past. Of course, the personalities, semantics, and settings change with time. Good watershed management is needed whether it is couched in terms of erosion control and agricultural production or in terms of water quality and human health. The approaches to solving problems are not likely to differ from those used in the past, either. That will remain true as long as districts function in the great American spirit that brought them into being and has guided them to this day.

2

Organization and Administration of Programs

Milton S. Heath, Jr.

Soil and water conservation services and programs in North Carolina are delivered by a combination of local, state, and federal agencies, along with a private association, by

- Local soil and water conservation districts
- The State Division of Soil and Water Conservation and the State Soil and Water Conservation Commission
- The U.S. Natural Resources Conservation Service
- The State Association of Soil and Water Conservation Districts
- The North Carolina Foundation for Soil and Water Conservation

The Three-Legged Stool

The activities of these agencies are so intertwined and interdependent that outside observers have trouble understanding just who does what. Even experienced insiders often fall back on a metaphor, "the three-legged stool," to describe this situation. Of course, everybody can appreciate that a three-legged stool won't stand up if you remove one of the legs.

Here are answers to some frequently asked questions.

1. How is soil and water conservation organized and administered at the local level?

As if to illustrate the three-legged-stool metaphor, the local districts in North Carolina (as in most states) were all created by a state agency,

Milton S. Heath, Jr., joined the Institute of Government faculty in 1957 and has specialized in conservation and environmental law and programs for over forty-five years.

the State Soil Conservation Committee (the State Committee), now known as the State Soil and Water Conservation Commission (the State Commission).

2. How are state soil and water programs organized and administered?

Creation of the local districts was initiated by a land-occupier petition, followed by a State Committee hearing and by the committee's final determination to create the district. [(See Section 139-5 of the North Carolina General Statutes (hereinafter G.S.).]

The boundaries of the original districts followed watershed lines, reflecting the philosophical preferences of early national soil conservation leaders. A later round of decisions by the North Carolina districts in the 1960s resulted in realignments of districts along county lines, as they now remain. (See Chapter 1.)

As of 2004 there were ninety-five single-county districts in North Carolina and one five-county district (Albemarle District, which covers Camden, Chowan, Currituck, Pasquotank, and Perquimans counties). All of the district supervisors serve four-year terms. The five-county district was created by the State Commission, which is still authorized by G.S. 139-4 to alter district boundaries upon petition from a district board or boards.

There are three elected supervisors in each county, including each of the five counties of the Albemarle District. All elected supervisors are chosen in non-partisan elections at the regular biennial fall election for county officers. There is no primary election for district supervisors.

In the five-county Albemarle District, two supervisors are appointed by the State Commission and spread among the five counties. (See G.S. 139-7, second unnumbered paragraph). In each of the remaining ninety-five counties, the State Commission appoints two supervisors.

ADMINISTRATION. The district is an independent unit of local government that functions, in keeping with Dr. Hugh Hammond Bennett's vision, as a bridge between the technical experts and private landowners. (See Chapters 1 and 4.) In the eyes of the law the district's board of supervisors is the district. The board is vested by law with all of the district's powers and duties, but it may delegate them to its employees or to individual supervisors. (See Chapter 5.) The district law is the legal foundation for these conclusions, but other state laws have an important influence on such basics as district financial management and personnel administration. (See Chapters 8 and 9.)

All of these matters will be explored in detail, beginning with Chapter 4.

3. How are state soil and water conservation programs organized and administered?

ORGANIZATION. At the state level the soil and water conservation program is the responsibility of the North Carolina Department of Environment and Natural Resources (DENR). The Governor appoints the secretary of DENR, who appoints the director of the Division of Soil and Water Conservation (the Division). The secretary also appoints the heads of the sections for district operations, technical services, non-point source programs, and administrative services. The Division head appoints area coordinators for each of the state's eight areas. The area coordinators work out of their area offices with the districts located in their areas. (See G.S. 143B-9.)

The policy and rule-making board for the state program is the seven-member State Soil and Water Conservation Commission. Three members of the State Commission are the president, first vice president, and immediate past president of the State Association of Conservation Districts. Three members are supervisors nominated at the annual meeting of the State Association in January from the three geographic regions of North Carolina and then appointed by the Governor. (One person is nominated each January.) One additional commission member—traditionally a supervisor—is appointed at-large by the Governor. All of the appointed members serve three-year terms. (See G.S. 143B-295.) Historically, the State Commission has been staffed by DENR.

ADMINISTRATION. A good way to look at the state's role with soil and water conservation districts is that the state helps keep the districts functioning in their independent roles as they carry out conservation programs and projects.

The state works with districts through the State Commission and the Division. The State Commission has the power, upon petition from a district or districts, to dissolve a district or change district boundaries. The commission also has the power to appoint supervisors to the district boards for appointed positions and assists with the legal process for elected supervisors. The commission can set policies for the districts on such matters as supervisor travel, the state cost share program, and district operations (such as developing long-range plans).

The State Commission helps coordinate state and federal resources from watershed projects to Clean Water Management Trust Fund Projects or 319 Nonpoint Source Pollution (NPS) Projects. The commission can also be the central point for coordination with other DENR divisions and agencies. In addition, the commission can provide direct resources to the districts, including funds for district operations, technicians to carry out NPS projects, cost-share funds, capability training and assistance with business plans, long-range plans, and cooperative agreements. The commission can establish rules, such as the Tar-Pamlico agricultural rules; enter into agreements for watershed projects (Public Law 566); or establish certifications on nutrient management and animal waste. When new opportunities arise, the commission can establish programs such as the Conservation Reserve Enhancement Program (CREP), community conservation programs, or conservation easements for districts.

The Division has a staff of approximately sixty resource people. Staff members vary from administrative personnel, who manage funds going to districts and board supervisors, to specialists, who assist districts with grants, non-point source pollution activities, the state's agriculture cost share program, watershed management programs, and engineering services. A district programs section provides area coordinators who are in direct contact with district staff and supervisors to offer assistance. In addition the Division also has a non-point source section that includes funding for 121 district technicians at the local level and a technical services section.

Districts can receive assistance from the Division for a wide range of things, including legal advice, supervisor appointments and elections, training, grant development, coordination with multi-district projects, questions from the board of supervisors or local governments, business plans, annual plans, and cooperative agreements. DENR also has other programs that may involve districts. These include .0200 Animal Waste Regulations, soils surveys, watershed planning programs, engineering projects, conservation easements, and erosion and sediment control programs. (The .0200 regulations are regulations of the North Carolina Environmental Management

Commission concerning wastes not discharged to surface waters, such as the animal waste management regulations codified as 15A N.C. Administrative Code, subchapter 2H, section .0200. See Chapter 4, Question 15, for further details on the ties of districts with state government.)

4. How are federal soil and water conservation programs organized and administered?

PROGRAMS. The Natural Resources Conservation Service (NRCS) of the U.S. Department of Agriculture and its predecessor agencies have been strong sources of technical advice and service to the local districts since the beginning of the soil conservation movement in the early 1930s. The NRCS traces its origins to the Civilian Conservation Corps camps that were assigned to conduct the erosion control projects inspired by Dr. Bennett. The success of the demonstration projects led to the creation of the Soil Erosion Service, which gave way to the Soil Conservation Service, and finally to the NRCS.

A succession of national farm bills have added cost-share payments and financial assistance to the technical services core of NRCS. Chapter 13 of this *Guidebook* describes the current programs that provide the local districts with a wide variety of choices to assist their land occupiers. The programs now available include

- Conservation compliance, sodbuster and swamp buster, introduced by the 1985 farm bill
- Conservation Technical Assistance (CTA), NRCS's largest conservation program for delivering technical assistance to support all USDA–related conservation programs
- The Conservation Reserve Program (CRP), with continuous sign-up for applying conservation practices in return for rental payments and with general sign-up during specified "sign-up periods"
- The Conservation Reserve Enhancement Program (CREP), an enhancement of CRP targeted to address significant water quality, soil erosion, and wildlife habitat concerns; in North Carolina this includes sensitive cropland and marginal pastureland in the Chowan, Neuse, and Tar-Pamlico basins and the Jordan Lake watershed

- The Environmental Quality Incentives Program (EQIP), which provides technical assistance, cost-share programs, incentive payments, and education to producers to address a number of soil, air, water, wildlife, and related natural resource concerns
- The Wildlife Habitat Incentives Program (WHIP), available on continuous sign-up to provide technical assistance and cost-share payments to landowners for restoration, development, and management of habitats such as native grasslands, pine savannas, and prairie remnants
- The Wetlands Reserve Program (WRP), which offers landowners easement and cost-share options to protect, restore, and enhance wetlands on their property
- Soil survey, based on the NRCS's leadership responsibility for the National Cooperative Soil Survey Program; North Carolina will soon have "once over" soil mapping completed statewide
- Resource Conservation and Development (RC&D), which seeks grant funding from non–USDA sources for community and economic development
- The Small Watershed Program, authorized by Public Law 566 of 1954 to provide technical and financial assistance to local governments, including the districts, to address localized flooding and drainage problems; the future focus of this program is likely to be mainly on rehabilitation of existing projects
- The Emergency Watershed Protection Program, which is the umbrella for technical and financial assistance for major natural disasters, such as hurricanes and other storms; during the 1990s NRCS provided $28 million in financial assistance to recover debris from clogged water courses and stabilize stream systems

ORGANIZATION. The U.S. Secretary of Agriculture appoints a state conservationist to serve as the chief executive of NRCS in North Carolina. The state conservationist, in turn, selects deputy state conservationists who provide technical service and guidance to the districts through area and district conservationists. Three NRCS areas now serve the State of North Carolina. In some local districts the NRCS district conservationist serves as the supervisor of technical services supplied in the district by local and state staff.

5. Where does the State Association of Soil and Water Conservation Districts fit in this picture?

For many years the districts have worked together collectively in a State Association, which is one of the strongest unifying forces for soil and water conservation in North Carolina. (The formal title is the North Carolina Association of Soil and Water Conservation Districts.) The State Association is not another unit of government but a voluntary association of all of North Carolina's districts.

The State Association was created to represent the districts' interests concerning conservation programs, financial support for conservation initiatives, and priorities and positions on public and regional issues. It provides a convenient way for all of the district supervisors, their spouses and their staffs to get together at an annual State Association meeting. The supervisors and their staffs also meet at fall and spring area meetings of the State Association in each of the association's areas on a regular schedule. The spring meetings usually occupy late February and March; the fall meetings, October and November.

The three-day annual statewide meeting in early January is a forum for developing recommended policies and recommendations for legislation through a committee system that sends its recommendations to the State Association meeting as a whole. The annual meeting is a major social, informational, and policy-making event to renew the inspiration of the conservation movement in North Carolina. The area meetings provide opportunities for training and for developing policy and legislative recommendations to be presented at the annual statewide meeting. Guest speakers are also invited to the area and annual meetings.

At the annual State Association meetings, the assembled supervisors elect officers for one-year terms—a president, a first vice president (who usually becomes the president a year later), a second vice-president, a secretary, and a treasurer. The president, first vice president, and immediate past president all serve on the State Commission, together with three supervisor members elected for three-year terms at the State Association meeting from the three major regions of the state. One of these three members is elected each year. (Technically, these three members are "nominated" by the State Association and formally appointed by the Governor, who also appoints an at-large member to serve as State Commission chair.) (See G.S. 143B-295.)

6. *What is the North Carolina Foundation for Soil and Water Conservation Districts, and how is it tied to the districts?*

The Foundation is a North Carolina charitable organization created to enlist financial support for districts primarily from the private sector. (Technically, it is a 501C-3 public, nonprofit, tax-exempt corporation. Donations to it are tax deductible.) The Foundation closely aligns itself with the work of the districts. It operates as a member of the conservation partnership in direct support of districts and the State Association.

An independent board of directors guides the Foundation. These directors come from all parts of the state and from many backgrounds including business, industry, agriculture, special interest groups, and organizations. They are a self-perpetuating board, meaning that they select their own members based on interest in the Foundation's purpose and a desire to work to gain support for district needs. The Association's president, immediate past-president, and first vice president sit as members of the board, assuring a constant connection between the Foundation and the districts. The board employs an executive director to handle the day-to-day business of the Foundation.

The Foundation focuses its work in three major areas of interest:

- Building capacity in conservation districts
- Educating the citizens
- Improving the natural environment

Some of the Foundation's early work has included a leadership development program for district supervisors, a project adding computers to district offices, this *Guidebook* for supervisors, and an initiative to support building outdoor environmental learning centers on school grounds. The Foundation has also added a program offering grants to districts for the closure of inactive lagoons and for related water quality projects on farms in the state. It is important for district supervisors to stay informed about the Foundation and let the directors know the districts' needs and priorities.

3

Before You Become a District Supervisor: Qualifications and Procedures

Milton S. Heath, Jr.

Do you want to become a district supervisor? This chapter tells you some of the things you need to know about seeking the office—before you throw your hat in the ring.

The word "office" is used by design, because a district supervisor probably holds a public office. For this reason we will review constitutional and statutory sources of qualification and disqualification for office. Before we address that subject, however, we will consider the procedure for supervisor election and appointment.

Supervisor Election and Appointment Procedure (Questions 1 through 3)

1. If you want to run for district supervisor, what is the procedure?
The steps that you must take in order to run for district supervisor are these:

- You must file a notice of candidacy with the county board of elections no earlier than noon on the second Monday in June and no later than noon on the first Friday in July preceding the fall election.
- You must pay a $5 filing fee at the time of the filing (take your checkbook or $5 in bills).
- If elected, you will take office on the first Monday in December following the election. At or before that time you need to take the oath of office. Ask an experienced supervisor for advice, or call the Division of Soil and Water Conservation, your Area Coordinator, or the Institute of Government.

Milton S. Heath, Jr., joined the Institute of Government faculty in 1957 and has specialized in conservation and environmental law and programs for over forty-five years.

- After the appointment of appointive supervisors (see Questions 2 and 3 in this chapter), the district board will select its officers. [See Section 139-6 of the North Carolina General Statutes (hereinafter G.S.)].

2. If you want to be considered for appointment as a district supervisor in one of the ninety-five single-county districts, what is the procedure?
The procedures for selection of appointive supervisors in the single-county districts are

- On or before October 31, as terms expire, the district board of supervisors recommends two persons from the district for appointment by the State Commission. If the names are not submitted as required for any county, the State Commission makes its own selections for that county.
- The State Commission makes its appointments prior to or at its November meeting, and the appointees take office the first Monday in December. At or before that time, the appointees need to take the oath of office. (See Question 1 in this chapter.)

3. If you want to be considered for appointment in the five-county Albemarle district that includes Camden, Chowan, Currituck, Pasquotank, and Perquimans counties, what is the procedure?
The State Commission, at its discretion and without local board recommendations, makes the appointments at the same time as it makes the other appointments, that is, prior to or at its November meeting. (See G.S. 139-7, first paragraph).

Qualifications and Disqualifications for Public Office (Questions 4 through 7)

4. Is a district supervisor a public officer?
There is no case law or statute that literally declares district supervisors to be "public officers," but it is very likely that the North Carolina courts would answer this question "yes." A test that is evolving in civil suits against local officials stresses four factors that are applied in determining that a person is a "public officer":

- The position is created by statute or constitution.
- The position has fixed duties that are prescribed by statute.
- The position holder exercises discretion in carrying out sovereign powers.

- The position holder takes the oath of office.[1]

It can be argued persuasively that all of these factors apply to district supervisors. It is a reasonable assumption that district supervisors are public officers, and we make that assumption in reviewing qualifications and disqualifications for service as a district supervisor.

5. What are the legal qualifications for serving as an elected district supervisor?

Article VI, Section 6 of the North Carolina Constitution declares that every qualified voter who is twenty-one years old shall be eligible for election by the people. From this we can reasonably infer that a person shall be at least twenty-one years old and a qualified voter in North Carolina in order to qualify for election as a district supervisor.

Who is a "qualified voter?" Anyone who has served as a precinct judge knows that the answer to this question can be difficult to pin down. Sections 1 and 2 of Article VI of the constitution specify several factors that might be considered in determining voter qualification:

- Being born in the United States or being a naturalized citizen.
- Residing in the state of North Carolina for one year and within the election district for thirty days next preceding an election.

6. Are there legal disqualifications for holding the office of district supervisor?

Article VI, Section 8 of the state constitution disqualifies "for office" (which would probably include appointed as well as elected district supervisors) persons who deny the being of "Almighty God"; persons not qualified to vote in an election for an elective office; persons adjudged guilty of a felony under the laws of North Carolina, another state, or the United States; and persons adjudged guilty of treason. G.S. 14-228 prohibits buying or selling offices or bargaining for an office.

---

1. Block v. County of Person, 141 N.C. App. 273, 540 S.E. 2d 415 (N.C. Ct. of Apps., 2001); EEE-ZEE Lay Drain Co. v. North Carolina Department of Human Resources, 108 N.C. App. 24, 422 S.E. 2d 328 (1992); Pigott v. City of Wilmington, 50 N.C. App. 401, 273 S.E. 2d 752, cert. denied 303 N.C. 181, 280 S.E. 2d 453 (1981).

7. What about dual office holding?
The constitutional dual-office-holding prohibition is an important lim-
iting factor for some present and potential citizen board members.
Article VI, Section 9 of the North Carolina Constitution prohibits concurrently holding (a) two elective offices or (b) any combination of
elective and appointive offices, except as the General Assembly provides by general law. The General Assembly has implemented the provision in G.S. 128-1.1 by authorizing any person to hold concurrently
(a) one elective office and one other appointive office or (b) two
appointive offices. The key to applying this provision, of course, is pre-
dicting accurately whether a particular position is a "public office."
(See Question 4 in this chapter.) In borderline cases it would be wise to
seek legal advice. Potential district supervisors should inform their
appointing officers of any local or state public office or position they
hold, so as to avoid the risk of inadvertently creating a prohibited dual
office. They should ask themselves the same questions before running
for office as an elected supervisor.

Sometimes when potential dual-office-holding problems arise, the district board can work with the Division of Soil and Water Conservation
and the State Commission to identify possible shifts of positions (from
elected to appointed or vice versa) that may solve the problems.

Legislation enacted in 2003 allows members of the State Soil and
Water Conservation Commission to hold that office in addition to the
maximum number of elective or appointive offices permitted to be
held by G.S. 128-1.1 [N.C. Sess. L. 2003-198 (H 727)]. This standard, however, does not create a new test for the office of district
supervisor.

Removal from Office (Question 8)
8. When can a district supervisor be removed from office?
When district supervisors show that they are no longer fit for office or
persistently neglect their duties, there is a remedy in the district law:
removal from office. G.S. 139-7 provides in its fifth paragraph that
any supervisor may be removed by the State Commission upon notice
and hearing "for neglect of duty, incompetence or malfeasance in
office, but for no other reason."

The difficulty of defining "neglect of duty" prompted the State
Commission to adopt a rule in 1986 (effective July 1, 1988) that evi-

dence of neglect of duty shall include, but is not limited to, ceasing to discharge the duties of office over a period of three consecutive months, "except when prevented by sickness" (15 N.C.A.C. 6A.0009). The rule directs the district boards to "advise the State Commission in writing of the failure of any supervisor to so discharge his duties over a three-month period."

4

The Basic Nature of Soil and Water Conservation Districts

Milton S. Heath, Jr.

This chapter is a primer on soil and water conservation districts in North Carolina. To simplify matters, we will use the word "districts" throughout to refer to soil and water conservation districts.

When you have read this chapter, you should have a working understanding of

- The origins and evolution of districts
- The relationship of districts to the legal system
- The basic nature of districts
- The District Law
- Laws, ordinances, rules, and policies
- The ties that districts have with federal, state, and local governments

The Origins and Evolution of Districts (Questions 1 and 2)

1. What are the origins of districts?

As described in Chapter 1, the idea of districts originated in the dust bowl era of the 1930s with Dr. Hugh Hammond Bennett of Anson County and other early conservationists. They recognized that local districts were needed to bridge the gap between technicians who would advise on methods of erosion control and private landowners whose cooperation would be required. By 1937 Bennett, while serving as director of the U.S. Erosion Control Service, persuaded President Roosevelt to recommend a standard district enabling law to the states.

Milton S. Heath, Jr., joined the Institute of Government faculty in 1957 and has specialized in conservation and environmental law and programs for over forty-five years.

North Carolina, like most states, enacted the standard district law and
began creating districts in 1937.

2. What has changed since 1937?
The early districts were soil conservation districts organized along
watershed lines, like Brown Creek District in Anson County (the first
district in the United States). There have been two notable changes
since those early days. First, all of North Carolina's districts are now
organized along *county* lines: ninety-five single-county districts and
one five-county district that includes Camden, Chowan, Currituck,
Pasquotank, and Perquimans counties. Second, all of the North
Carolina districts are now *soil and water* conservation districts, reflecting the growing emphasis on water conservation in district programs.

The North Carolina terminology is not standard throughout the
United States. In other states, districts go under various names, most of
which include the words "conservation" or "conservancy" in their titles.

Districts and "the District Law" (Questions 3 through 8)

*3. What is the District Law and what is its significance to districts and
district supervisors?*
We in the conservation movement often refer to "the District Law."
The District Law is Chapter 139 of the North Carolina General
Statutes (hereinafter G.S.), enacted in 1937 and amended a number of
times. It is the source of authority for creation of districts. Without Ch.
139 there would be no districts. It is important for district supervisors
to keep legislative support alive for the district law and for funding of
district programs.

4. If you want to change the District Law, how do you do it?
Bills to amend any statute or adopt a new statute must be introduced by a
legislator and enacted by the General Assembly. Usually, the best way for
districts to get legislation enacted is to develop proposals in the fall and
get them approved by the State Association at its January annual meeting.
This allows time for bills to be drafted that can be filed in time to meet
legislative deadlines. A good example is the legislation concerning liability
of districts that was approved at the January 2001 State Association
meeting, introduced by Representative Arlie Culp and enacted by the
2001 General Assembly. (See Chapter 12 of this *Guidebook*.)

5. Where do you find the District Law?
District supervisors who have attended the Institute's basic school have been given copies of the District Law and related legislation in their school books. District offices that do not have a copy of the District Law can obtain one from the Institute. You can also ask the Division of Soil and Water Conservation or your area coordinator about its availability on the Internet or as a separate pamphlet.

6. When you find the District Law, what should you do with it?
You should read it! Your oath of office requires you to know the law, and your constituents expect it of you.

7. When you find the District Law, what is in it?
Among the important provisions of the District Law are

- The procedures for creation and modification of districts.
- Some of the important powers of districts.
- Some of the legal duties of districts.
- Some procedures that govern the way the District Board functions.
- The Watershed Improvement law.
- A formula for state grants for small watershed projects.

8. Does the District Law contain all of the law that concerns districts?
No it does not. Some state laws impose legal duties on all units of government, including Soil and Water Conservation Districts. Other state laws are enabling laws that grant counties powers that are of interest to some districts. Still other state laws directly address the work of some districts.

Examples of state laws that impose duties on districts and other units of government are

- The Open Meetings Law, which applies to the meetings of the district boards and of the State Commission
- The Public Records Law, which applies to records of districts and the State Commission
- The Local Government Budget and Fiscal Control Act, which governs district budgets and audits (see Chapters 7 and 8 of this *Guidebook*).

Examples of state enabling laws of interest to districts are the drainage district law and the county service district and special assessment laws, which offer alternative methods of financing drainage and flood damage prevention projects. (See General Statutes Chapter 156; G.S. 153A-185 to 153A-206; and G.S. 153A-300 to 153A-310.)

Examples of state laws that directly address the work of districts include

- The Sedimentation Pollution Control Act, which permits districts to comment on erosion control projects (G.S. 113A-60 to 113A-61)
- The Agriculture Cost Share Law and other laws relating to nonpoint source pollution and animal waste management (see Chapter 5 of this *Guidebook*)
- The amendment to the state conflict-of-interest statute that limits the application of that statute to district supervisors under some circumstances (see Chapter 5 of this *Guidebook*)

These and other state statutes of concern to districts have been included in the school book for the Institute's annual basic training course for district supervisors. They reflect the need for district supervisors and staff to be familiar with a number of state statutes in addition to the district law itself. They are available on the Internet and may be accessible at district offices.

The Basic Nature and Status of Districts (Questions 9 and 10)

9. *What is the legal status of a soil and water conservation district?*
Under the District Law (G.S. 139-8) a district is "a governmental subdivision of the state and a public body corporate and politic," with a list of standard corporate powers:

- To sue and be sued
- To enter agreements and contracts
- To acquire property
- To make studies, develop plans, and carry out projects

In these respects, a district resembles a county, which in North Carolina is identified in G.S. 143A-11 as a "body politic and corporate;" is often called a "subdivision" of state government; and has a list of corporate powers similar to a district's powers.

Under G.S. 150A-11 a city or town is a "municipal corporation" with similar corporate powers. Under more general legal principles, should districts be considered "municipal corporations"? Quite possibly, though the district law does not use that term.

Other North Carolina laws use general terminology that has been interpreted as including districts and district boards, such as

- The district is considered a "local government" or "unit of local government" or "public authority," in the Local Government Budget and Fiscal Control Act, G.S. 159-7(b)(10) and (15).
- The district board is considered a "public body" under the Open Meetings Law, G.S. 143-318.10(b).
- The district is an "agency of North Carolina government or its subdivisions" under the Public Records Law, G.S. 132-1.

Districts are also "conservation districts" under the federal farm bills.

Taking into account all of this terminology, it seems clear that districts are independent units of local government similar to other special districts or public authorities, and resembling counties and cities. A district is literally a "governmental subdivision" and "public body corporate," and it may well be a municipal corporation in the eyes of the law. The precise legal nature of districts will probably not be clear until established by court decision.

10. Are districts part of federal, state, or county government?
All North Carolina districts work closely with and rely on the federal and state governments, and most districts have strong connections with their county governments. At various times these ties have been so close that some observers have thought that districts were really part of the federal, state, or county governments. Is this in fact the case?

Despite these close ties, the best answer is probably "none of the above," as a matter of statutory interpretation. The evidence is persuasive that districts are and always have been independent units of local government, in keeping with Dr. Bennett's vision of the local district as a bridge between technical experts and private landowners.

Laws, Ordinances, Rules, Policies (Questions 11 and 12)

11. By the way, what are laws, ordinances, rules, and policies?
A dictionary definition of "law" is a set of standards that guide our conduct in society and that is enforceable by public agencies—enforceable, for example, by criminal prosecutions or by injunctions against violations.

When we speak of "the law," we mean the entire body of law or a segment of the law, such as "federal law." (Of course, we may also use "the law" as a slang term for the police.)

In common usage, a "law" is a statute enacted by the United States Congress or a state legislature.

An "ordinance" is a formal document adopted by a town council or board of county commissioners that is the local government's equivalent of a statute enacted by the Congress or a state legislature. Some other local boards, such as local boards of health, also have the authority to adopt legally binding rules. Most ordinances and state or federal rules and statutes are legally binding documents that have the force of law.

A "rule" is a formal regulation adopted by an administrative agency, such as the United States Environmental Protection Agency or the North Carolina Wildlife Resources Commission. At the local level in North Carolina, local boards of health have the authority to adopt enforceable rules. (See G.S. 130A-39.)

The word "policy" has no settled meaning comparable to the settled meaning of a law or an ordinance or a rule. "Policy" is used in different ways by different people. Sometimes people refer to "a policy" as if it were a synonym for a law, an ordinance, or a rule.

A more limited meaning of policy is: a concept or guideline that is not adopted in the form of a binding law, ordinance, or rule. In this sense, districts, the State Commission, the State Division, and NRCS can all have policies on a variety of subjects for the management of their programs.

12. Just exactly where do rules fit into the legal system?
Most legislators realize that they cannot anticipate all of the questions that will arise under legislation, and they may delegate to administrative agencies the responsibility to adopt rules that will address these details. (In this sense, "rule" is a synonym for "regulation." In North Carolina today all of the agency rules and regulations are usually referred to as "rules," and the process of adopting them as "rule-making.")

Are rules of this kind "law" and part of "the law"? Yes, if they are legally enforceable. Most of the rules adopted by regulatory agencies such as the Environmental Management Commission are enforceable, and they are part of the law.

If you are a district supervisor, you might ask the question "How about the rules of the State Soil and Water Conservation Commission?" That commission is directed by G.S. 143B-294(2) to "adopt rules consistent with this chapter." Those rules "shall be enforced by the Department of Environment and Natural Resources." Does this make State Commission rules enforceable law, even though no statute makes violations of those rules a crime or enjoinable? There is no easy answer to this question, because rules of the State Commission don't quite fit the pattern of typical rules, for example, of the Environmental Management Commission.

Ties between Districts and Federal, State, and County Governments (Questions 13 through 15)

13. What are the ties of districts with the federal government?
Relationships between districts and other levels of government sometimes are so strong that they blur the lines between organizations. The districts' ties with the federal government originated in the dust-bowl-era work of Dr. Bennett of the U.S. Soil Erosion Service (later, the Soil Conservation Service). His work proved the value of applied technical knowledge in addressing soil erosion problems. Dr. Bennett's genius in linking local districts with the furnishing of technical know-how to private landowners was the origin of a constructive working relationship between districts and the technicians of the U.S. Soil Conservation Service (SCS)—recently renamed the Natural Resources Conservation Service (NRCS).

From the late 1930s into the 1960s, SCS provided the great majority of staff support to the district program, mainly by providing technical staff to assist cooperating landowners. As local district programs expanded and became more diversified, districts—working through their county governments—secured funding to hire secretarial/clerical assistance. Many districts started with part-time assistance, but most districts now have full-time clerical positions that provide support to the entire partnership.

The 1970s and 1980s brought new challenges to districts, especially in the area of water quality. There was a clear need to accelerate technical assistance to cooperating landowners beyond the level that could be provided by SCS staff. Once again, districts rose to the occasion and began hiring technical staff to work alongside SCS staffers. For the most part, funding for this acceleration was again provided by county governments. The approval of the N.C. Agriculture Cost Share Program in the mid 1980s greatly accelerated the hiring of technical staff by districts through matching funds provided by the state.

Growth of district staffing only strengthened the relationship with the federal government and NRCS specifically. NRCS continues to have primary responsibility for the technical part of the district program to include creation and maintenance of technical standards and specification, technical training to both NRCS and district employees, and technical quality assurance.

In some districts the NRCS district conservationist may supervise some of the local staff, although NRCS is limited by its own rules in the supervision that it can provide to non-federal employees. NRCS also brings to the districts a continuing connection with developments at the national level that augments the resources that districts can make available to their constituents. A succession of national farm bills beginning in 1985 has made available to districts through NRCS a variety of cost share payments and financial assistance. (See Chapters 2 and 13 of this *Guidebook*.)

14. *What are the ties of districts with state government?*
The very existence of districts is linked to the legislative branch of state government, the General Assembly. Districts were created pursuant to legislation enacted by the General Assembly—the District Law. What the General Assembly gives it can take away. The District Law could be repealed by the General Assembly, and it can be (and has been) amended. Districts need to keep their fences mended with their state senators and their state representatives, so that these elected legislators will not forget the importance of the district law and of legislative support to the districts.

Districts have strong *organizational* ties with state government, both historical and ongoing. First, the approval of a state board—the State Soil Conservation Committee—was required to establish each original district. (The State Committee was the predecessor of the current State Soil and Water Conservation Commission.)

Second, the State Soil and Water Conservation Commission is the chief policy-making body at the state level for soil and water conservation in North Carolina and appoints two of each district's supervisors. (This commission is one of the state boards in the Department of Environment and Natural Resources.) The District Law goes as far as a law can go to ensure that the state commission will remain in close touch with the grass roots of soil and water conservation by providing that six of the seven members of the commission are active district supervisors (G.S. 143B-295). In actual practice, all of the members of the State Commission have been district supervisors, because the seventh member (an at-large appointee of the Governor) has always been a district supervisor.

Third, the state commission is staffed by one of the divisions of the Department of Environment and Natural Resources (DENR), the Division of Soil and Water Conservation. The division gives districts a working link to state government. It oversees several state programs that are important to districts, including Agriculture Cost Share, Small Watershed, and District programs. The area coordinators, who work closely with the districts in their areas, are employees of the division.

Fourth, the districts benefit from a state budget that helps to support a number of district activities. The state soil and water conservation budget is recommended by DENR and the Governor and is adopted by the General Assembly. (Translation: It is important to stay on good terms with all of them.) District interests that have benefited by the state budget in recent years include

- Per diem compensation of district supervisors for attending meetings
- Partial salary support for some local district staff
- Funding of the agricultural cost share program
- State grants for small watershed projects, as funds are made available by the General Assembly

Fifth, the districts are authorized by the District Law to call upon the North Carolina Attorney General's Office, for such legal services as they may require (G.S. 139-7). A series of assistant or deputy attorneys general, including Dan Oakley and (currently) Ryke Longest, have taken this responsibility very seriously and provided excellent legal services to the districts and the division. (See discussion on pages 90 and 109 on the role of county attorneys as legal advisers to districts.)

The style of state–district relations has varied over time, just as the style of federal–district relations has varied. Until the reorganization of North Carolina government in the early 1970s, soil conservation was not technically a part of state government. The State Committee was usually served by a single staff member whose office was located on the campus of North Carolina State University. And outstanding staff they were, indeed—first Bryce Younts and later Jack Smith.

State government reorganization brought soil and water conservation into state government as a division within the predecessor department of DENR. The division grew moderately in numbers of staff during the 1970s, but it did not become a strong player in the department until Dr. Joseph Phillips became head of the division in the early 1980s. Dr. Phillips' imagination and his leadership abilities helped to develop the agricultural cost share program, which spread from a three- or four-county project to a statewide program that made cost share payments totaling $5 to $10 million available to all of the districts. In the 1990s the division's profile within the department was lifted another notch by the vigorous leadership of Dewey Botts and David Vogel. Close ties between State Commission chair James Ferguson with the office of Governor James Hunt helped to cement the division's role in state government. All of this eventually generated apprehension among some of the leaders of the state association of districts about the state–local balance, which has led to a renewed emphasis within the conservation movement on the importance of districts.

15. What are the ties of districts with local governments?
At the local level districts are closely tied with local governments—especially their county governments—in several ways. Some county governments began supplying districts with office space and part-time secretarial assistance soon after the first districts were organized. In recent years a number of counties have become much more involved in staff support for districts. In some districts the employees supported by the counties are "county employees" in every sense; in others they are "district employees." (See Chapter 9 of this *Guidebook*.)

A majority of the district supervisors are elected by the voters of the county at the same elections as county commissioners. The plus side of this is that elected officials can often make common cause. An election may be an opportunity for the supervisors who are running for office to develop or strengthen ties with county commissioners for the benefit of their districts. If there is a "down side" to this equation, experienced supervisors may be able to help those who are new to running for office recognize any risks that may be involved.

District and county budgets and audits are governed by the same statute, the Local Government Budget and Fiscal Control Act (G.S. 159, Article 3). A number of districts have chosen to turn their budgeting and audits over to their counties in order to take advantage of the established budget and audit machinery of the counties. (See Chapter 5 of this *Guidebook.*)

Most districts attract important resources into their counties, such as cost share payments and support of small watershed projects. It is important for district supervisors to tell their county commissioners and county managers about these things, so that they will be aware of the benefits that soil and water conservation bring to their counties. Ask your area coordinator for current information on these benefits.

5

Powers and Duties of Soil and Water Conservation Supervisors and Districts

Milton S. Heath, Jr.

This chapter provides an overview on the legal powers and duties of soil and water conservation districts and supervisors in North Carolina. As you read this chapter, keep in mind some basic ideas.

First, in the eyes of the law the districts and the board of supervisors are one and the same, for most purposes. The District Law often uses the words "district" and "district board" interchangeably. Some sections of the District Law, such as Section 139-8 of the North Carolina General Statutes (hereinafter G.S.), grant general powers to the districts and the district boards. Other sections, such as G.S. 139-9 and 139-12, grant certain powers simply to the board of supervisors.

Second, the District Law authorizes the district board to delegate its legal powers and duties to others, such as employees or individual supervisors. (See Question 5 in this chapter for details.) In other words, the law does not artificially require the district board to act formally as a board on each and every one of its program responsibilities.

Third, most of the district's legal *powers* are found in the District Law, collected mainly in G.S. 139-8. Some of the district's legal *duties* are found in the district law, such as in G.S. 139-7. Some of the district's most important legal duties, however, are found in other statutes, such as the Open Meetings Law, the Public Records Law, and the Local Government Budget and Fiscal Control Law.

Milton S. Heath, Jr., joined the Institute of Government faculty in 1957 and has specialized in conservation and environmental law and programs for over forty-five years.

After reading this chapter you should have a working understanding of the following subjects:

- The district's powers and duties
- Some important limitations on those powers and duties
- The sources of the district's powers and duties
- How the district's powers and duties can be delegated to others

Organization of This Chapter

This chapter covers several relatively simple topics, as well as one large and complex topic: powers to help districts deliver conservation programs. In order to move from the simple to the complex, the topics in this chapter are organized in the following order:

- Definitions
- Legal duties of districts
- Corporate and administrative powers of districts
- Legal powers to help districts deliver conservation programs
- How districts and the conservation movement in North Carolina can continue to adapt to change in the conservation landscape.

Definitions (Question 1)

1. What are "powers and duties"?
Since we are considering district powers and duties, what are "powers" and "duties"?

A *legal power* of a district is authority that may be exercised at the discretion of the District Board of Supervisors. An example is the district's power under G.S. 139-8 (4) to acquire real property—enabling authority that the district *may,* but is not required to, exercise.

Statutory grants of power are often expressed by the word "may." For example, the fourth paragraph of G.S. 139-7 gives the district the power to ask the Attorney General for legal assistance. It provides that "the supervisors *may* call upon the Attorney General . . . for such legal services as they may require."

A *legal duty* of a district is a legal obligation of the district board of supervisors that is mandatory, not discretionary. For example, the last paragraph of G.S. 139-6 provides that "It shall be the duty of the district board of supervisors . . . to develop annual county and district goals and plans for soil conservation work therein . . ."

Statutes often use the word "shall" to impose a legal duty. For example, the fifth paragraph of G.S. 139-7 states that "The supervisors *shall* provide for the execution of surety bonds for all employees and officers who shall be entrusted with funds or property." (Notice that the second "shall" in this sentence does not express a legal duty. It is merely a use of the word "shall" as a synonym for the words "is" or "are" or "will be.")

Depending on the context, the violation of a legal duty by a public official may be a criminal offense, may be enforceable by an injunction, or (as a practical matter) may be simply a political obligation.

Legal Duties of Districts

Duties Imposed by the District Law and Other Laws (Questions 2 and 3)

2. *What legal duties are imposed on districts by the District Law?*
FINANCIAL DUTIES. G.S. 139-7 imposes some limited *financial duties* upon the district supervisors that need to be read with the more comprehensive mandates of the Local Government Budget and Fiscal Control Act (see Chapter 8 of this *Guidebook*). Under G.S. 139-7 (fifth unnumbered paragraph) the supervisors are required

- To provide for the execution of surety bonds for all officers and employees entrusted with funds or property.
- To provide for an annual audit of the amounts of receipts and disbursement during the year. G.S. 139-7 allows the supervisors to provide for a simplified "informal audit" instead of the more detailed formal audit required by the Local Government Budget and Fiscal Control Act. (See Chapter 8 for details.)

ADMINISTRATIVE DUTIES. G.S. 139-7 also imposes some limited *administrative duties* upon the district supervisors. It requires the supervisors to designate a chairman and to keep a full and accurate record of their proceedings and of all resolutions, regulations, and orders that they adopt (third and fifth unnumbered paragraphs of G.S. 139-7). It also requires the supervisors to furnish copies of their ordinances, rules and regulations, orders, contracts, forms, and other documents to the State Commission, on request.

DUTY TO DEVELOP PLANS AND GOALS. G.S. 139-6 requires the district board "to develop annual county and district goals and plans for soil conservation work therein."

DUTIES UNDER THE SMALL WATERSHED LAW. Article III of the District Law, often referred to as the Small Watershed Law, covers watershed improvement programs of counties. Under this law counties have several options for implementing county watershed improvement programs. One option is to designate the county's soil and water conservation district to carry out the program on behalf of the county. If the county so designates the district, the district supervisors have the following statutory duties under G.S. 139-41(d) and (h):

- To provide the board of county commissioners a proposed budget thirty days prior to July 1 for the upcoming fiscal year.
- To provide the county commissioners with and publish an audit within sixty days after expiration of a fiscal year ending on June 30.
- To determine the qualifications of its watershed employees, officers, agents, and consultants.
- To provide for the execution of surety bonds for the secretary-treasurer and others entrusted with funds or property.

The audit requirement for small watersheds does not specifically authorize use of a simplified "internal audit," as under G.S. 139-7. It is possible that the county would accept an "internal audit" if this were specified in the operational agreement between the district and the county. (See Chapter 14 of this *Guidebook*.)

G.S. 139-41.2(d) requires that the county submit a proposed method of operation for watershed works to the State Commission in conjunction with its watershed work plan. This duty would devolve on any district board designated to carry out a county's watershed program.

3. What legal duties are imposed on districts by statutes other than the District Law?
Important legal duties are imposed on districts by several other statutes and rules. These include the Open Meetings Law, the Public Records Law, and the Local Government Budget and Fiscal Control Act. (See Chapters 7 and 8 of this *Guidebook* and Question 9 in this chapter.)

General Powers of Districts

Corporate and Administrative Powers (Questions 4 and 5)

4. What general corporate powers are conferred on districts?
The District Law also confers general corporate powers on districts in G.S. 139-8 that may be exercised in connection with any district programs and activities. These include the power to

- Sue and be sued in the name of the district.
- Have perpetual succession.
- Have a seal.
- Make and execute contracts and other instruments.
- Make, amend, and repeal rules and regulations not inconsistent with Chapter 139 to carry into effect its purposes and powers. (The District Law does not expressly empower districts to enforce its rules and regulations by criminal prosecution for violations or by seeking injunctive relief in the courts.)
- Acquire real or personal property by purchase, exchange, lease, gift, bequest, devise, or otherwise; to obtain options upon property; and to sell, lease, or otherwise dispose of its property.

These corporate powers are codified in G.S. 139-8(a)(4) and (9).

5. What administrative powers are conferred on districts?
In G.S. 139-7 the District Law confers some general administrative powers upon districts.

PERSONNEL POWERS. The district supervisors may employ a secretary, technical experts whose qualifications are approved by the N.C. Department of Environment and Natural Resources (DENR), and such other employees as they may require (fourth unnumbered paragraph of G.S. 139-7).

LEGAL SERVICES. The supervisors may call upon the North Carolina Attorney General for such legal services as they may require (fourth unnumbered paragraph of G.S. 139-7).

LOCAL COOPERATION. The supervisors may invite any of their local legislative bodies (county commissioners or town councils) to designate a representative to advise and consult with the supervisors on questions affecting their interests (sixth unnumbered paragraph of G.S. 139-7).

AUTHORITY TO DELEGATE. The district supervisors "may delegate to their chairman, to one or more supervisors, or to one or more agents, or employees such powers and duties as they may deem proper" (fourth unnumbered paragraph of G.S. 139-7). Good practice suggests that each district board adopt one or more resolutions that delegate any powers the board desires to delegate, to be recorded in the board's minutes.

Conservation Program Powers

North Carolina's Conservation Landscape

When the North Carolina General Assembly first passed the District Law in 1937, the state's conservation needs and the number and function of federal, state, and local agencies were vastly different from what they are today. That model landmark legislation and its 1959 Small Watershed amendments established a state and local partnership with the federal government to protect and restore soil and water resources and to assist private landowners in using conservation practices. This partnership has formed the backbone of highly successful efforts over the past sixty-seven years to address serious national problems in soil erosion, flood damage, and water quality.

Since 1937, however, North Carolina has seen the establishment of new federal, state, and local government agencies or departments to deal with protection of natural resources and otherwise regulate landowners' activities. These new regulatory agencies (e.g., the U.S. Environmental Protection Agency, the N.C. Department of Environment and Natural Resources and its attendant commissions, and county environmental programs) have acquired broad authorities and responsibilities—in some cases similar to those outlined in the soil and water conservation statute. As in many states, the role of the districts and the state commission in helping landowners manage private lands was somewhat eclipsed as these new agencies developed and expanded their specific regulatory authorities and responsibilities. While the soil and water conservation statute provides very broad *authorities*, specific *responsibilities* in many of those same areas are assigned to other, newer agencies or commissions.

Like most states, North Carolina's emphasis on regulation, and the responsibilities assigned to the Environmental Management Commission and other commissions, has led to a command-and-control approach in dealing with landowners. Under such an approach, the contribution and significance of voluntary programs through soil and water conservation districts and the conservation partnership can begin to erode unless careful attention is focused on maintaining the proper role for non-regulatory programs and the financial support within the state for local conservation programs. Fortunately, the General Assembly has maintained good support for conservation programs, including funding for the Agriculture Cost Share Program, supervisor travel, and district matching funds. The General Assembly has tried, with some success, to use conservation programs to assist landowners and agricultural procedures in meeting their obligations associated with regulatory programs.

Despite this fact, supervisors in many of North Carolina's ninety-six soil and water conservation districts have trouble relating their general statutory authorities to today's resource protection landscape. If unchecked, this uncertainty can result in the supervisor's role becoming one of follower rather than leader, as conservation agencies hesitate to meet new landowner or community needs, and as regulatory agencies and commissions enact top-down federal or state mandates for landowners. District supervisors need to understand how their district law provides authority to meet the modern needs of landowners and citizens in natural resource protection and conservation.

Today, our landowners, agricultural producers, and communities are faced with a host of regulations and programs dealing with their use of private lands. These include controls on alteration of lands, on water sources and water management (e.g., retention, storm water, disposal), erosion control, agronomic practices, wetlands protection, wildlife management, and others. The state itself has become a major landowner, with the goal of acquiring one million acres through a precedent-setting land purchasing program. As these programs and regulations are developed, locally based voluntary efforts to help landowners manage private working lands often do not receive due recognition, nor do the benefits of locally based partnerships with private landowners or local input on acquisition and management of publicly owned lands.

Fortunately, today's political and economic landscape provides opportunities for soil and water conservation districts and their partners to become more important participants in natural resource protection programs and in private and public land management decisions. The

1996 Farm Bill expressed a theme of "Locally Led Conservation" that has its roots in the leadership of local soil and water conservation as part of the national farm and environmental policy. These are important actions in reaffirming the role of soil and water conservation districts in serving the state's landowners and agricultural producers and in redirecting priorities in farm programs. At the same time, state initiatives in land and water conservation depend on a substantial increase in local leadership; they provide opportunities for soil and water conservation districts to assume a larger local role in important statewide conservation and resource protection issues.

The District Law encourages cooperation among districts (G.S. 139-12) and encourages districts to invite county and municipal governing boards to designate representatives to consult with district supervisors on mutual interests (G.S. 139-7, sixth unnumbered paragraph). The district law also directs the state commission to coordinate district programs and to secure cooperation and assistance from federal and state agencies with districts (G.S. 139-4).

To take advantage of these opportunities, districts must adapt their programs and plans to meet these new challenges. To become leaders in local efforts, supervisors must first understand the powers and responsibilities of soil and water conservation districts, and how the "well-worn" powers and approaches authorized under the conservation statute can fit into today's landscape for conservation—a landscape reshaped since the conservation statute was first passed in 1937.

Powers Granted by the District Law to Help Districts Deliver Conservation Programs to Landowners and Others (Questions 6 through 8)

SMALL WATERSHEDS

6. What powers are granted in the District Law (G.S. 139) to help districts deliver conservation programs?
In the original 1937 legislation, the district was given a broad array of planning and implementation powers to address soil conservation and erosion control issues. The 1959 Small Watershed Law expanded the scope of these powers to also cover flood prevention, and the conservation, utilization, disposal, and development of waters. Subsection (a) of G.S. 139-8 spells out the district's powers in delivering these programs to

   a. Conduct and publish surveys and investigations.

b. Construct and maintain structures, works, and projects.
c. Carry out preventive and control measures and works of improvement.
d. Cooperate and enter agreements with agencies and land occupiers, including agreements to furnish financial aid.
e. Develop comprehensive plans.
f. Act as agents of the United States in connection with acquisition, construction, operation, and administration of projects.
g. Make available machinery, equipment, fertilizer, seed, and seedlings to land occupiers within the district to carry out conservation operations on their lands.
h. Require contributions in money, services, or materials from those who benefit from work on lands not owned by the state.
i. Require land occupiers to enter agreements or covenants concerning the permanent use of their lands to control erosion, flooding, and sediment damages.
j. Assist the State Commission in implementing and supervising the Agriculture Cost Share Program for non-point source pollution control and other DENR programs to protect water quality.

This is a mouthful, but every supervisor needs to be aware of these powers. It may be helpful to break this listing down into more manageable groupings.

Some of the items in this list overlap one another, such as the powers to carry out projects and works of improvement under paragraphs (b) and (c). Some of the items describe steps that can follow one another in sequence—for example, the investigation and planning powers in paragraphs (a) and (e) are natural first steps toward carrying out the powers concerning projects and works in paragraphs (b) and (c).

Some of these powers are basically there to facilitate various district programs—the powers listed in paragraphs (d) and (f) through (j) fall in this category—that is, the powers to enter agreements, act as agents of the United States, make machinery and supplies available, require contributions, require land use agreements, and assist in cost-share programs.

7. What about the Small Watershed (P.L. 566) Program?
The Small Watershed (or Watershed Improvement) Program assists farmers and other local residents with flooding, farmland drainage,

and related water conservation problems. The typical piedmont or mountain project may involve one or more small impoundments that provide for water storage to control flooding, a sedimentation pool, and downstream channel clearance. It may also include limited storage for water supply and recreational use, as well as areas for conservation of fish and wildlife habitat. Eastern North Carolina projects usually emphasize drainage improvements rather than flood prevention. (The reference in the Small Watershed Law to "disposal of water" has enabled districts to move into drainage projects as well as flood prevention.)

Individual small watershed projects are usually carried out either by counties acting under G.S. 139-41 or by drainage districts acting under Subchapter III of G.S. 156. (At one time Article II of the District Law also authorized watershed improvement districts to be created to sponsor small watershed projects, but this authority was repealed in 1993.) Federal aid is authorized by Public Law 566 and state aid by Article IV of G.S. 139. Actual federal and state funding depends on appropriations by Congress and the North Carolina General Assembly, which vary from year to year and have diminished in recent years.

The District Law provides the necessary powers to take part in small watershed activities in several ways, as follows:

- G.S. 139-8 grants to the districts the power to plan and carry out projects for flood prevention, development of water resources, floodwater and sediment damage reduction, and utilization and disposal of water—taken together, the substance of small watershed projects.
- G.S. 139-41 grants to county commissioners the same set of powers, with or without the support of a referendum-based watershed improvement tax of up to twenty-five cents on the $100 valuation.
- Under G. S. 139-41, a county that undertakes a small watershed program may operate it directly, create a watershed improvement commission, or designate its soil and water conservation district to carry out the program.
- Soil and water conservation districts, cities, and counties may also participate in small watershed projects by contributing

funds to specific features (such as water supply) or serving as cosponsors. (See G.S. 139-41 and 139-48.)

There have been no "new starts" of small watershed programs in districts for many years, but some planned structures remain to be built or completed. An important area for new work when funds are available is repair and renovation of structures to meet federal and state dam safety requirements. Another opportunity for new work when funding permits is raising structures above flood levels as an alternative to building new structures.

LAND USE

8. Does the district have the power to regulate land use?
The answer to this question is both "yes" and "no."

It is "yes" in that districts are empowered by G.S. 139-9 to adopt land use regulations governing the use of land within a district with approval by a two-thirds majority of a land-occupier referendum vote. Districts can enforce these regulations pursuant to G.S. 139-10 and 139-11.

The scope of these regulations is limited by G.S. 139-9 to conserving soil and water resources and preventing soil erosion. A list of specific requirements that may be included in the regulations covers engineering operations, methods of cultivation, cropping programs, tillage practices, and retirement of erosive lands from cultivation.

It is "no" in the sense that no district has actually adopted land use regulations. A few districts have considered the possibility, but they have not adopted regulations because of certain built-in obstacles. Among these obstacles are the two-thirds approval requirement, the lack of established referendum procedures, and the lack of supervisor experience in conducting referenda. Ultimately, the philosophic resistance of many farmers and other rural residents to regulation may be the biggest obstacle of all.

To put this matter in its larger context, a number of voluntary programs have developed that cover much of the same territory without imposing land use regulations. These programs range from agriculture cost sharing to the various federal initiatives that assist districts. (See the next question and Chapter 13 of this *Guidebook*.)

Powers Granted by Other Laws (Question 9)

9. What powers are granted by statutes other than the District Law to help districts deliver conservation programs?

AGRICULTURE COST SHARE PROGRAM FOR NON-POINT SOURCE POLLUTION CONTROL

First, the Agriculture Cost Share Program for Non-point Source Pollution Control, created by G.S. 143-215.74, operates under the supervision of the State Soil and Water Conservation Commission. The program is designed to encourage conservation practices within districts that will have the greatest impact in improving water quality. It has grown in coverage from a handful of counties in 1985 with designated nutrient-sensitive waters to, potentially, all of North Carolina's counties, if they apply for funds.

The State Commission annually allocates funds appropriated by the General Assembly to districts that participate voluntarily for distribution by the districts to participating farmers who meet the State Commission's designated priorities. State funding may not exceed 75 percent of the average cost for each practice, with the assisted farmer providing 25 percent of the cost, either in dollars or by in-kind support—$75,000 is the annual maximum payment that may be made to each applicant.

Two sections of the District Law make district supervisors and members of the State Commission eligible to receive cost-share payments without violating the state conflicts of interest law (G.S. 14-234), if certain conditions are met. Cost-share payments may be made to a district supervisor who does not vote on the application or attempt to influence the outcome, and the application is approved by the State Commission as well as the district board. Cost-share payments may be made to a State Commission member if the member does not vote on the application or attempt to influence the outcome and if the application is approved by the secretary of DENR as well as the district board.

Another statute, G.S. 143-215.74B, established a special rules agency committee to review the Agriculture Cost Share Program periodically. This committee consists of the commissioner of Agriculture and Consumer Services, the master of the State Grange, the president of the Farm Bureau Federation, the deans of the agriculture schools at North Carolina State University and North Carolina Agricultural and

Technical State University, the chair of the State Commission, the president of the State Association, and the directors of Wildlife Resources and Marine Fisheries or their designees.

SEDIMENTATION POLLUTION CONTROL

Second, Article 4 of G.S. Chapter 113A enacted the Sedimentation Pollution Control Act of 1973, which established a state program to impose "minimum mandatory standards which will permit development of this State to continue with the least detrimental effects from pollution [of the waters of this State] by sedimentation" (G.S. 113A-51). The act authorizes cities and counties to establish their own local erosion control programs with the approval of the Sedimentation Control Commission. In recent years there have been thirty to forty active local programs approved by the Commission.

Under G.S. 113A-61 the Commission may require that any local program submit copies of erosion control plans to their soil and water conservation districts for review, comments, and recommendations within twenty days of receipt of the plan (or a shorter period if agreed upon by the district and the local government). Failure to submit timely comments does not delay final action on the plan.

COUNTY SUPPORT OF DISTRICT PROGRAMS AND OF RELATED ACTIVITIES

Third, Counties are authorized by G.S. 153A-44D to cooperate with and support the work of districts, and to appropriate for these purposes revenues not otherwise limited as to use. Counties are also authorized by G.S. 153A-440.1 to establish, maintain, and finance county watershed improvement programs, drainage projects, and water resources development projects. In addition to these general authorizations, counties are authorized to provide financing for several types of projects that are of interest to districts, as follows:

- By levying county special assessments for watershed improvement, drainage and water resources development projects under G.S. 153A-185 to 153A-204.1
- By creating county service districts for any of the above purposes and levying property taxes within any such district to finance the activity (G.S. 153A-302;307)

Counties are also expressly authorized by legislation enacted in 2001 to provide for the legal defense of any district supervisor or soil and water conservation employee (whether a county or district employee) and to pay a damage claim or judgment against a district supervisor or employee. (See G.S. 153A-97 and 160A-167.)

Limitations (Question 10)

10. What are the limitations on the district's powers?
The district is not a general-purpose local government like a city or county. Among other things, it has no taxing powers and no condemnation powers. (Under the Small Watershed Law a county may acquire property by condemnation, however, with the approval of the State Commission.) Districts have no regulatory enforcement powers—that is, no authority to adopt ordinances enforceable by law.

Sometimes districts may need access to these general purpose authorities. Districts that maintain good working relationships with their county and city officials will be better able to call on them to exercise general government powers for the benefit of districts.

Federal Laws (Question 11)

11. What powers do federal agencies (such as NRCS) have to help districts deliver conservation programs?
This rather large subject requires a separate chapter in this *Guidebook* —see Chapter 13.

Adapting to Change in the Conservation Landscape

The soil and water conservation movement has a solid record of adapting to changes in the conservation landscape of North Carolina. The district supervisors of the past played a crucial role in the movement's evolution since the enactment of the District Law in 1937. Today's district supervisors can play a similar role in adapting to change in the twenty-first century. Indeed, the supervisors *must* play a strong role in present and future adaptations if the movement is to thrive in the years ahead.

The Record of Past Adaptation (Question 12)

12. How have the districts and the soil conservation movement adapted to change since the enactment of the District Law in 1937? Chapter 1 of this *Guidebook* traces the detailed history of soil and water conservation in North Carolina since 1937. This section highlights some of the ways in which the conservation movement has responded to change imposed by circumstances and has proactively initiated change.

EXPANSION OF THE PROGRAM TO INCLUDE WATER CONSERVATION. The leadership of North Carolina's conservation movement reflected a growing awareness that soil erosion could not be fully addressed in isolation from water conservation when it asked the legislature to rename "soil conservation districts" as "soil and water conservation districts" in 1961. (See N.C. Session Laws 1961, Chapter 744.) Renaming the districts completed the legislative circle begun by Congress when it enacted Public Law 566 in 1954 and by the North Carolina legislature when it enacted the Small Watershed Law in 1959. (See N.C. Session Laws 1959, Chapter 781.)

BROADENING THE WATER CONSERVATION PROGRAM TO COVER WATER QUALITY MANAGEMENT. The Small Watershed Law focused on structural measures to "hold the water on the land" and to abate recurring agricultural floods. In the early 1980s North Carolina conservationists led by Dr. Joseph Phillips pioneered measures that broadened this water *quantity* focus to include water *quality* enhancement. Beginning with nutrient reduction efforts in the Chowan River Basin, our districts with the support of state agricultural and environmental leaders developed the concept of agriculture cost sharing for non-point source pollution control that has since spread to cover the state in a multimillion dollar annual program. (See Question 9 in this chapter.)

MOVING FROM LAND USE CONTROL TO THE AGRICULTURE COST SHARE PROGRAM. The development of the Agriculture Cost Share Program also represents a fresh start from unworkable provisions of the original District Law concerning land use regulation for erosion control. Three sections of the 1937 District Law gave districts the authority on paper to control soil erosion by adopting enforceable land use regulations with referendum approval by land occupiers of the district (G.S 139-9 to 139-11). No North Carolina district has ever implemented these provisions,

for a combination of reasons, including the unworkability of the referendum procedure and the incompatibility of this regulatory machinery
with the voluntary philosophy of the conservation movement. It
remained for the Agriculture Cost Share Program to rescue erosion control from an unworkable beginning in G.S. 139-9 to 139-11 and to
broaden it to cover water quality as well as soil conservation.

RESPONDING TO THE ONGOING URBANIZATION OF NORTH CAROLINA.
It is common knowledge that continuing urbanization has transformed
North Carolina from its rural small-town origins to an increasingly
urbanized-suburbanized state in the twenty-first century. Districts that
are most impacted by this transformation are responding to this chal-
lenge by evolving programs that offer a broad menu of service to
urban and suburban dwellers as well as the farm population. In some
districts the selection of some urban and suburban district supervisors
has helped facilitate this evolution of district programs.

WORKING LANDS CONSERVATION. In recent years districts have par-
ticipated with other local governments and nonprofit organizations in
acquiring land for conservation or preservation. Supervisors who
attended the 2004 annual meeting of the State Association were
treated to a morning of presentations that explored a growing emphasis on "working lands conservation" combined with acquisition of
conservation easements rather than transfers of fee ownership. The
working lands program offers opportunities to achieve preservation
and conservation without taking active farmland out of production.

ALIGNMENT OF DISTRICTS WITH COUNTIES. The districts have
strengthened their base of support by becoming more closely aligned
with counties, in a series of steps:

- North Carolina's original districts were created with watershed
  boundaries. In the 1960s the districts' boundaries were redrawn
  to be coterminous with county lines.
- Beginning in the 1980s, a majority of the districts have come
  under the county budget and audit processes, taking advantage
  of established county fiscal arrangements.
- County funds help support growing numbers of district personnel
  and operations. The districts reciprocate by bringing agriculture
  cost-share and other payments to the residents of their counties.
  Some district staffs are organized as county departments.

- A strong district employees association has been developed and its programs expanded. (See Chapter 10 of this *Guidebook*.)
- District-county political ties have been strengthened since the early 1970s by bringing the election of district supervisors into the fall elections where county commissioners and legislators are elected.

ALIGNMENT OF DISTRICTS WITH STATE GOVERNMENT. North Carolina districts have strengthened their ties with state government in a series of steps over the years:

- In the early 1970s the State Committee on Soil and Water Conservation was renamed a "State Commission" and brought into a cabinet department (DENR and its predecessors), as part of a general reorganization of state government.
- The inclusion of the State Commission in DENR has given soil and water conservation access to a cabinet secretary and related departmental programs, to a departmental budget, and to potential staff growth that could not have been imagined under the previous organization. (The DENR Division of Soil and Water Conservation now numbers sixty resource people. See Chapter 2 of this *Guidebook*.)

STRENGTHENING OF THE STATE ASSOCIATION AND CREATION OF THE NORTH CAROLINA FOUNDATION FOR SOIL AND WATER CONSERVATION. The North Carolina Association of Soil and Water Conservation Districts has been a significant force in the conservation movement since the 1940s. Its activities have been expanded into a regular program of spring and fall area meetings. Leaders of the State Association have also organized an allied charitable agency, the North Carolina Foundation for Soil and Water Conservation, created to enlist financial support for the districts from the private sector. The Foundation has raised over $2 million in a few years for projects such as a leadership development program for district supervisors, this *Guidebook* for supervisors, installation of computers in district offices, and a grant program to support closure of inactive animal waste lagoons. (See Question 5 in Chapter 2 of this *Guidebook* for details.)

CONCLUSION. This review of the evolution of soil and water conservation in North Carolina since 1937 reflects the dynamic character of the movement and its adaptability to changing conditions for nearly seventy years. This record of continuing vitality is a good omen for the future of soil and water conservation in North Carolina in the twenty-first century.

Using the District's Basic Statutory Powers in the Years Ahead (Question 13)

13. How can the districts draw upon their statutory powers to deliver conservation programs in the twenty-first century?

SUPERVISOR ROLES AND RESPONSIBILITIES IN A MODERN SOIL AND WATER CONSERVATION DISTRICT. It is the responsibility of the soil and water conservation district supervisors to provide the consensus leadership at the local level to make decisions regarding the community's natural resource priorities and to determine how best to meet local natural resource needs through cooperation with landowners and partnering organizations. This is the role for soil and water conservation districts as envisioned by their enabling legislation in 1937, as well as by the 1996 Farm Bill theme for Locally Led Conservation. A fundamental role for the board of supervisors is to bring together at the local level all interested and affected parties, together with the support organizations charged with providing technical and administrative assistance, to develop and implement a plan to address the community's natural resource concerns.

Through a locally led consensus process, or the community conservation approach, supervisors help to identify and determine priorities for conservation programs and work with partners to implement programs that provide assistance to landowners, agricultural producers, local residents, and local government units. It is not necessary for a soil and water conservation district to possess all the resources needed to implement conservation programs. Districts have access to expertise and resources of their federal and state partners and should rely in part on partners' cooperation and assistance in meeting local priorities. However, supervisors should seek to develop local technical and financial resources within a district, to the degree feasible, to expand the numbers and types of tools in the "conservation toolbox" and to expand the district's capabilities to deliver local conservation programs.

HARNESSING THE DISTRICT'S BASIC POWERS TO THE TASK AHEAD. Based on today's conservation landscape, supervisors should apply the powers and authorities of soil and water conservation districts in new and innovative ways to accomplish this basic role. Supervisors must seek new ways to work with traditional partners, and they must establish new partnerships with other organizations—both state and local—to fill modern roles.

Fortunately, looking again at powers and responsibilities contained in the District Law (see Question 6 in this chapter), supervisors can see a solid framework for supporting these modern roles. Six specific examples of a district's modern role can be shown:

1. TO CONDUCT SURVEYS, INVESTIGATIONS, AND RESEARCH ON CONSERVATION, AND CONDUCT DEMONSTRATIONS. As national and state initiatives place greater reliance on use of nonregulatory programs to meet the challenges of water quality protection statutes (e.g., federal AFO/CAFO regulations), they create an *increased demand* for local technical assistance services, local demonstration projects which show the effectiveness of conservation practices, and local programs that provide tracking and follow-up with producers on the use of best management practices (BMPs). For example, district cost-share activities partly fall under the category of providing demonstration (through the use of incentive payments and cost sharing) of improved conservation practices. (The careful reader of the statute, G.S. 139-8, may observe that it does not expressly refer to "demonstrations." Those familiar with the conservation movement will recognize, however, that from its New Deal origins under Dr. Bennett, soil and water conservation has been essentially an extended exercise in "demonstration.")

   Because of their unique relationship with local landowners and the conservation partnership, soil and water conservation districts and agricultural extension agencies are the *only* organizations that can perform these activities *as a service* to landowners without regulatory connections.

2. TO DEVELOP COMPREHENSIVE PLANS FOR CONSERVATION OF SOIL AND WATER RESOURCES. The recent federal Clean Water Action Plan and the Unified National Strategy for Animal Feeding Operations illustrate how important comprehensive conservation

planning has become. Federal and state initiatives place an extraordinary demand on nutrient management planning, conservation planning, engineering, construction, cost share, irrigation management, and other practices. North Carolina has active state programs dealing with animal waste management and nutrient-sensitive waters that incorporate conservation planning to protect water quality. Soil and water conservation districts play an important role in preparation, review, and approval of plans, and in follow-up with landowners to determine how well their plans are working and identify and correct operational problems. These services represent a critical and doable role for soil and water conservation districts, provided sufficient resources are made available.

3. **TO CARRY OUT PREVENTIVE AND CONTROL MEASURES AND WORKS OF IMPROVEMENT FOR CONSERVATION ON PRIVATE LANDS OR PUBLIC-OWNED LAND, WITH THE COOPERATION OF LANDOWNERS OR THE PUBLIC LAND MANAGEMENT AGENCY.** Today, soil and water conservation districts carry out such measures as part of a partnership with the private or public landowner, where the district helps make resources available to private landowners for technical and financial assistance (cost share, for example) for conservation measures, or provides management services for publicly owned lands. The need for this role has never been greater in North Carolina as it is under recent federal Farm Bill legislation and new state initiatives for water resource protection.

The state's initiative for preserving one million acres provides new opportunities for district participation in policies and programs related to public land acquisition and management, and for expanding the role of less-then-fee mechanisms (e.g., conservation easements) to help accomplish goals for conserving natural resources while retaining land in private ownership. Furthermore, the community conservation initiative will create new opportunities for districts to assist their local governments (counties and municipalities) in conserving and managing publicly owned land.

4. TO MANAGE PROJECTS AS AGENTS OF FEDERAL OR STATE AGENCIES AND TO ACCEPT CONTRIBUTIONS IN MONEY, SERVICES, OR MATERIALS FROM FEDERAL OR STATE AGENCIES IN CARRYING ON ITS OPERATIONS. This long-standing responsibility has been employed to assist in projects such as flood control, erosion control, and emergency watershed restoration (EWP). Under this component, districts accept funding and other assistance from the state General Assembly and Congress (via NRCS). This provision has implications for districts as the General Assembly considers changes to the state's erosion and sediment control programs (e.g., local delegation) and to the state's wetlands and stream restoration program, and as the state ramps up its programs for preserving important natural resource lands and habitats through public land acquisition and management. This provision allows soil and water conservation districts to undertake new management opportunities, and to accept funding in the process.

The Division of Soil and Water Conservation's active participation in water quality and water policy issues has expanded district exposure to critical state and federal water resource protection issues. These efforts are bringing soil and water conservation districts together with new partners (i.e., other DENR divisions, local land trusts, private river associations) to participate in solutions to issues on water quality and land management. As these new roles are identified, the Division and the Association are working together to provide technical and financial assistance to soil and water conservation districts, through legislation, grants, contracts, and training.

5. TO COOPERATE AND ENTER INTO AGREEMENTS WITH PUBLIC AGENCIES AND LANDOWNERS IN CONSERVATION ACTIVITIES. This authority may be used to develop agreements with new and existing partners. These agreements may include public/private partnerships; agreements for land management services (e.g., holding conservation easements); agreements for critical water conservation issues (e.g., water conservation practices and water use efficiency under the Coastal Plain Capacity Use Area Plan or

establishing mobile irrigation laboratories); developing agreements for district participation in the state's stormwater program; and promotion of innovative agricultural equipment and practices for soil conservation, and water retention and management, soil and plan testing, animal products testing, public education, and other services. Agreements may be developed with state (e.g., DENR divisions), regional, and local agencies, and private landowners.

It is a supervisor's responsibility to help recognize potential partners for such arguments, and to take steps to reach out to form new partnerships. Supervisors can look to the state's area coordinators and NRCS personnel for guidance in these matters. Soil and water conservation districts offer new partners valuable local allies in natural resource conservation and management efforts.

6. **TO INVITE LOCAL GOVERNMENT (MUNICIPAL OR COUNTY) REPRE-SENTATIVES TO ADVISE AND CONSULT WITH THE DISTRICT ON ISSUES THAT AFFECT LOCAL PROPERTY, WATER SUPPLY, OR OTHER INTERESTS.** This communication is a critical link to educating local government about the local benefits of soil and water conservation programs, and in maintaining local support and contributions to district programs. Supervisors should keep close and productive contact with their local elected counterparts. Model local agreements are available upon which to base a cooperative relationship with a municipal or county government. It is a supervisor's responsibility to cultivate these local relationships and to educate local government about how the soil and water conservation district can help meet local needs.

Examples of key local interests that can be met with the help of districts include new local stormwater requirements for education, post-construction stormwater control, and erosion and sediment control; innovative use of incentive-based programs to apply buffers for water quality; local/state collaboration on farmland preservation, water use efficiency and conservation, local water supply planning protection of water supply sources, comprehensive land use planning, and local educational programs. In North Carolina, counties provide over $10 million in contributions to districts, through matching funds for technical positions, operating expenses, office space, vehicles, and other support. Traditional district programs for cost-share programs and technical assistance to local landowners can be expanded to round out a comprehensive local conservation program. Supervisors should make local governments aware of federal and state funding available at the local level, as well as other value-added benefits a district may provide through partnership in conservation programs.

These six examples illustrate how a soil and water conservation district can apply its powers and duties to meet today's challenges. Supervisors should consider these and other opportunities in developing their business plan for district activities.

6

How to Run an
Effective Meeting

Milton S. Heath, Jr.

The district board meeting is a place where many decisions can be
made to guide districts in their programs. The same is true of the State
Soil and Water Conservation Commission (the State Commission). It is
important that district boards and the State Commission run effective
meetings in a businesslike and timely way. The meetings should be
interesting to supervisors and citizens.

Area coordinators and others who have observed district board
meetings know that many district board meetings are consistently well
run, but others are not. This chapter assembles a few basic ideas and
suggestions for effective board meetings that involve good preparation,
agendas, the actual meetings, and follow-up.

1. What preparations should be made for board meetings?
The chair should prepare meeting agendas with staff assistance and
input from other supervisors. Or staff may prepare agendas after con-
sulting with the chair or the board. The agenda should be set early
enough to allow time for preparation of any backup material, but late
enough to include items that might not be ready to include at an early
date. (See Figures 6-1 and 6-2 for examples of meeting agendas.)

a. It is helpful to break the agenda down into categories such as
announcements, the consent or information agenda, the suspense
agenda, and the action agenda. You need a regular agenda format that
will become familiar to all.

Milton S. Heath, Jr., joined the Institute of Government faculty in 1957 and has specialized in conservation and environmental law and programs for over forty-five years.

Figure 6-1. Agenda Format

Estimated
Time

7:00 p.m.   Announcements
- By the chair: a request for supervisors to state any known conflicts of interest or appearance of conflicts
- By supervisors
- By staff

7:10   Petitions and requests
- Public
- Supervisors
- Staff
(This refers to petitions requesting action by the board.)

7:15   Consent agenda: A list of agenda items that will be deemed approved unless a supervisor requests any item be removed or "pulled" from the consent agenda for an explanation and possible formal board action. The consent agenda might include things like staff reports on various items, or information developed by staff for the board.

7:20   Approval of minutes (on supervisor's motion)

7:25   Regular agenda
- Items for board action
- Items for discussion only, preliminary to actions at a future meeting
- Any closed session items, such as personnel actions that may be considered in closed session

Figure 6-2. Sample Agenda

District Soil & Water Conservation District
and
Duplin Watershed Improvement Commission

Duplin County Social Services Building, Kenansville, NC

April 8, 2002
8:00 a.m.

1. Call to Order
2. Welcome—Introduction (board members)
3. Approval of Minutes—March 4, 2002, meeting
4. Informational Items
   A. Lagoon Closure Program update
   B. Federal programs update
   C. Education programs update
   D. Envirothon volunteers needed
   E. 2002 Program Objectives of the N.C. Association of Soil & Water
      Conservation Districts
   F. Notification of S&W Commission electing to continue funding third
      cost share technical position through December, 2002, contingent
      upon availability of technical assistance funds
5. Action Items
   A. N.C. Agriculture Cost Share Program
      1. Requests for payment:
      a. Mitchell Paige   31-02-03-02   3 Year Cons. Tillage (236.7 Ac.)
         $14,202
      b. Bennie Paige   31-02-04-02   3 Year Cons. Tillage (227.0 Ac.)
         $13,620
      c. Dwight Sholar   31-01-21-02   WSS-Poultry $15,000
      d. Joey Brinkley   Swine Buyout Program (Filter Strips—Trees)
         $1,509
   B. Supplemental allocation of contingency funds/request
      1. New contracts:
      a. Charles Rhodes   31-02-13-02   Livestock Exclusion (Pending)
         $8,989
      2. Fifty-three current year applications on hand for funding (plus or
         minus $500,000)

(continued on page 64)

Figure 6-2. Sample Agenda (*continued*)

---

6. Conclusion
   A. Comments
   B. Remarks by the chairman
7. Next regular board meeting—May 6, 2002 at 7:30 p.m.—
   Districts/NRCS Office Building
8. Adjourn

---

b. The chair can open the meeting by asking if staff or other super-visors have any announcements. The *action agenda* is simply the items that are ready for board action at that meeting.

c. A *suspense agenda* is a device that can be helpful in planning meeting agendas. This will ensure that items needing timely attention are listed on the agenda. Such items might include meetings leading up to the State Association of Conservation Districts annual meeting and area meetings, the annual budget meeting (see Chapter 2), preparation and approval of the cost-share program strategy plan, handling cost-share spot checks, memoranda of understanding with the county and the state and the Natural Resource Conservation Service (NRCS), annual performance reviews of non-federal local staff, preparation for annual events (contests, environmental soil stewardship month, and so forth), and any other matters anticipated to require later board action.

d. A *consent* or *information* agenda offers two alternative ways to present information to a board without necessarily requiring board debate and action concerning individual items on that agenda. Some boards use an *information agenda* that allows staff or others to speak to the board about matters of interest. Other boards are given written information in a *consent agenda* package that the members can read in advance of a meeting. The supervisors can then be prepared to ask questions or make comments at the meeting if they wish. A supervisor who has a question about a consent agenda item can ask the chair to "pull" that item from the agenda in order to allow that question to be raised. If there are no questions, the entire consent agenda can be approved by unanimous consent on the motion. If there is a question about one item, the rest of the consent agenda can be approved by unanimous consent.

Each board can choose for itself whether to use the information agenda or the consent agenda, or it can choose one approach sometimes and the other sometimes. The consent agenda can save meeting time if the staff has time to prepare backup materials in advance of the meeting. The information agenda usually requires more meeting time, but this may not be a problem for some boards.

e. Prior preparation for board meetings is essential for successful meetings. Both staff and supervisors need to prepare:

- Staff, by preparing resource materials in time for supervisors to review before the meeting
- Supervisors, by reviewing the agenda package before the meeting so that they will be ready to discuss the business of the meeting

The agenda and all supporting resource materials should be made available to supervisors five to seven days prior to a meeting.

f. Staff or the chair needs to keep supervisors informed of special meetings and committee meetings, if there are any.

g. The chair is responsible for the requirements of the Open Meetings Law, such as complying with advance notice requirements, having a meeting room that will accommodate interested visitors, and satisfying the Open Meetings Law's provisions on closed meetings. (See Chapter 7.)

2. *What about the meetings themselves?*

a. A specific person (staff or the secretary of the board) should be assigned responsibility to keep minutes of board meetings, which will be part of the agenda package. Minutes should be recorded in a clear, concise form. Minutes should reflect all aspects of decisions by the board—who made the motion, who seconded the motion, and the results of the vote. There should be a designated custodian of the official copy of the minutes, such as the secretary of the board.

b. The board should decide what rules of parliamentary procedure will be followed during meetings and adopt a motion recording this action. Do you rely on *Robert's Rules of Order* or some other standard set of rules (such as the Institute's *Suggested Rules of Procedure for*

Small Local Government Boards by A. Fleming Bell, II)? If Robert's is the guide, there are various editions, and the board should decide which one to follow. There are some differences from edition to edition that might be important to you.

c. Meetings should start and end on time. The chair is responsible for the conduct of the meetings. Above all, meetings should be kept interesting and timely.

Here are a few ideas:

- Be on the lookout for and invite interesting speakers. This can help keep the board abreast of new technology and emerging issues. It also might provide an opportunity to invite legislators or county commissioners to speak to the board and socialize with supervisors.
- Area coordinators might regularly share information with the district boards about interesting meeting topics of other district boards.
- Identify informed observers who would be willing to sit in on some of your board meetings and make suggestions to staff or boards.

3. What else should we keep in mind?
You might keep these thoughts in mind:

- Should the board adopt bylaws? (Area coordinators might provide sample bylaws and agendas.)
- The bylaws or a resolution should spell out the board's officers, terms, and selection procedure.
- The bylaws or a resolution should spell out procedures for going into and coming out of closed sessions.
- What are the most important things that a district board does, other than adopting a budget and developing proposals to area meetings and the annual meeting of the State Association? Should these things be reflected in agenda planning, and the like?
- What should the relationship be between staff and board? If there isn't a fair degree of consensus on this important question, it may be difficult to have an effective board.

7

Laws That Impose Legal Duties or Restrictions on a District: The Open Meetings Law and The Public Records Law

Milton S. Heath, Jr.

This chapter addresses two important state laws that impose legal duties on district boards and the State Soil and Water Conservation Commission (the State Commission)—the Open Meetings Law and the Public Records Law. Every district supervisor and district or state soil and water employee should know the basic requirements of these laws. Noncompliance with either of these laws has serious consequences for districts and soil and water conservation personnel.

When you have read this chapter you should have a working knowledge of

- The coverage of the North Carolina Open Meetings Law and the Public Records Law.
- The requirements and procedures that these laws impose on districts, on the State Commission, and on the State Division to hold open meetings and to allow citizen access to their files for documents that are "public records."
- The legal consequences of failing to observe these laws.
- Procedures for purging and managing public records.

For a complete treatment of these issues, see David M. Lawrence, *Public Records Law for North Carolina Local Governments* (Chapel Hill, N.C.: The University of North Carolina at Chapel Hill, Institute

Milton S. Heath, Jr., joined the Institute of Government faculty in 1957 and has specialized in conservation and environmental law and programs for over forty-five years.

of Government, 1997), and David M. Lawrence, *Open Meetings and Local Governments in North Carolina*, sixth edition, revised (Institute of Government, 2002).

References in this chapter are to both Lawrence, *Public Records*, and Lawrence, *Open Meetings*.

Section 1: Open Meetings Issues for Districts and the State Commission

Coverage and Requirements of the Law (Questions 1 through 4)

1. Are the district boards and the State Commission subject to the requirements of the North Carolina Open Meetings Law?

Yes, both the district boards and the State Commission are covered by this law [Chapter 143, Article 33A of the North Carolina General Statutes (hereinafter G.S.), titled "Meetings of Public Bodies"]. It applies to any public body. The term "public body" includes any state or local board or commission that

- Has two or more members, and
- Is authorized to exercise legislative, policy-making, quasi-judicial, administrative, or advisory functions.

The district boards and the State Commission obviously meet this test. (G.S. 143-318.10.)

2. What does the Open Meetings Law require?

It requires (with a few exemptions) that "each official meeting of a public body shall be open to the public, and any person is entitled to attend such a meeting." [See G.S. 143-318.10(a).]

The result is that unless a particular district or State Commission meeting is exempted (see Question 8 below), all of these meetings must be open public meetings, where anyone who wants to may attend. As a matter of common sense, this means that meeting rooms must be large enough to accommodate the sort of public attendance that is likely to occur.

3. By the way, what difference does it make whether you comply with the Open Meetings Law?

It makes two important differences. *First*, a violation is illegal. Anyone can take a violator to court and get a court order declaring the actions taken at a meeting null and void, and issuing an injunction against further violations. Short of an injunction or a null-and-void order, the court could simply find that a violation has occurred. (See G.S. 143-318.15, 143-318.16.)

Second, the media (the press, radio, and television) are the main guardians of the Open Meetings Law. You are almost guaranteed to get bad publicity if you violate this law and it comes to the attention of the media.

4. What are the main things that the Open Meetings Law requires districts and the State Commission to do?

First and foremost, the district board, State Commission, and their subcommittees must do public business in an open way. If you always keep this basic requirement in mind, and proceed accordingly, you will be in compliance with the spirit of the Open Meetings Law. (See G.S. 143-318.9.)

Second, you must give public notice of your meetings in the manner specified by the law. (See G.S. 143-318.12.)

For *regular meetings*, you must keep on file a *current* notice in a central place. For districts, the "central place" is with the district's clerk and with the clerk to the board of county commissioners. (The law is ambiguous on this point, and it is best to file in both places to be on the safe side.) For the State Commission, the "central place" is with the Secretary of State. If the schedule changes, the schedule must be filed at least seven calendar days before the first meeting under the new schedule.

For *special meetings* at a time *or* place other than the regular meetings, two notices are required. One is a notice posted at your bulletin board (if you have one) or at the door of your meeting room. The other is by mail or fax or delivery of notice to anyone who has filed a written request for it. Both notices must be given at least forty-eight hours in advance of the meeting and state the time, place, and purpose of the meeting. If the forty-eight hours' posting period occurs over a weekend, be sure to post the notice where it can be seen, not in a closed building.

For *emergency meetings*, you only must notify any local news media that have requested notice. (A good example of an emergency meeting is a special meeting that can't comply with the forty-eight-hours notice requirement.) As a general practice it's a good idea to keep your local media informed of all your meetings.

For *recessed meetings*, you need give no further notice if the original meeting was properly noticed. When you have meetings lasting more than a day that include flexible subcommittee meetings, it may be useful to "recess" your meetings (instead of "adjourning") to the next scheduled time and place.

Third, committee meetings are separate official meetings for purposes of the Open Meetings Law. Be sure that your committees each comply separately with the law. [See G.S. 143-318.10(b).]

Fourth, the Open Meetings Law prohibits secret ballots at a public meeting. Written ballots are allowed only if signed ballots are made available for inspection in your clerk's office immediately following the meeting. [See G.S. 143-318.13(b).]

Fifth, the Open Meetings Law allows the news media to tape or broadcast your meetings, subject to reasonable regulations. (See G.S. 143-318.14.)

Sixth, you can meet by conference call if you comply with the notice requirements and give the public an opportunity to hear. (Some local boards have rooms set up for this purpose, with loud-speaker systems.) You can charge a fee of up to $25 per listener to help defray the cost of the location and equipment. [See G.S. 143-318.13(a).]

Seventh, any "official" meeting of a majority of the district board of supervisors is subject to the Open Meetings Law. ("Official" meetings include meetings to conduct a hearing, deliberate, take action, or otherwise transact public business. "Deliberate" includes acquisition and exchange of information, as well as discussion. It would include briefings, workshops, and board interviews of job candidates, as well as collective discussion at a board meeting.) Although the statute allows "social gatherings" that are not "official meetings," this cannot be used to camouflage discussion. (Lawrence, *Open Meetings*, questions 17, 18, 20, 21, 22, 23, and 28.)

Meetings of Other Groups (Questions 5 through 7)

5. What about meetings with other boards or groups?
Meetings with other boards, such as the board of county commissioners, are subject to the Open Meetings Law if you are doing district business. Also subject to the law are district board meetings with private groups where you are engaged in any part of the process of deliberating on district business and "retreats" or field trips where official district business is considered. (See Lawrence, *Open Meetings*, questions 17 through 28.) Consult with the Division of Soil and Water Conservation if you need advice on these matters.

6. Does the Open Meetings Law apply to meetings of the State Association?
No, the State Association is not a "public body" within the meaning of the Open Meetings Law.

7. Does the Open Meetings Law apply to area meetings?
Again, no. The area organization is not a "public body" within the meaning of the Open Meetings Law. However, if a district board attending an area meeting holds a meeting, it is subject to the Open Meetings Law. In addition, a district board must obtain the approval of the director of the Division of Soil and Water Conservation to hold a meeting outside its county.

Exemptions (Question 8)

8. You mentioned "exemptions" from the Open Meetings Law. What are they?
There is a list of exceptions in G.S. 143-318.11 that allows a public body to adopt a motion at an open meeting to hold a closed session dealing with a subject listed in G.S. 143-318.11(a). The motion must state the purpose of the closed session. Only the board members have a *right* to attend a closed meeting, but the board may *allow* others to attend. (See Lawrence, *Open Meetings*, Question 69.)

Topics eligible under G.S. 143-318.11 for a closed session of potential interest for districts include the following.

- THREE TYPES OF PERSONNEL MATTERS that the board may consider. First, its negotiating position concerning compensation

and other terms of an existing or proposed employment contract; second, a present or prospective employee's or officer's
"qualifications, competence, performance, character, fitness,
conditions of appointment, or conditions of initial employment;" and third, a complaint, charge, or grievance by or against
an individual officer or employee.

- ATTORNEY-CLIENT CONSULTATIONS. The board may consult at a
closed meeting with its attorney in order to preserve the attorney-
client privilege. (Examples include discussion of liability issues
and negotiations by the attorney with others.) It may consider
and give instructions to its attorney concerning handling or set-
tling of a claim, a suit in court, an administrative proceeding, or
an arbitration or mediation.
- PRIVILEGED INFORMATION. At a closed meeting the board may
address information that is privileged or confidential under state
or federal law—such as medical records—in order to prevent
disclosure.
- REAL PROPERTY ACQUISITION. At a closed meeting the board may
consider the district's negotiating position concerning acquisition of real property (but not personal property).
- INDUSTRIAL SITES. At a closed meeting the board may consider
location or expansion of a business or industry.
- CRIMINAL INVESTIGATIONS. At a closed meeting the board may
plan, conduct, or hear reports concerning investigation of
alleged criminal misconduct.

Records and Minutes (Questions 9 and 10)
9. What records must be kept of meetings?
The Open Meetings Law requires the board to keep minutes of
both closed meetings and open meetings. It also requires the board
to keep a "general account" of any closed meeting, so that people
who were not there could have a "reasonable understanding" of
what transpired. The general account probably should at least identify the subject of the meeting and briefly summarize the discussion.
It need not identify the positions taken by particular individuals.
Both the minutes and the general account may be in the form of a
written narrative or an audio or video recording. [See G.S. 143-
318.10(e).]

10. Must the minutes or general account be available for public inspection under the Public Records Law?

The Open Meetings Law allows the minutes or general account of a closed session to be withheld from public inspection for "so long as public inspection would frustrate the purpose of the closed session." The answer to this question, then, depends on the purpose of the closed session and the content of the minutes and general account. For example, it wouldn't frustrate the purpose of the closed session to open for inspection an account of an instruction to an attorney to purchase land once the deed has been done, but it would frustrate the purpose of a closed session to open for inspection privileged information. (See Lawrence, Open Meetings, questions 144 and 145.)

If you need more information on the Open Meetings Law you can buy a detailed guide from the Institute of Government (David M. Lawrence, *Open Meetings and Local Governments in North Carolina*, sixth edition, revised 2002). It would probably be useful for each district to keep one copy of this guide for reference in your office and at your meetings. The guide is updated and reissued periodically. It includes the text of the law and a list of common questions and answers (similar to the questions and answers in this chapter) written by the Institute's specialist on open meetings, who drafted the original act.

Section 2: Public Records Law Issues for Districts and the State Division

The North Carolina Public Records Law lays down a general rule that public records are subject to public inspection and copying. (See G.S. 132-6.) Here are some basic questions on the coverage and requirements of this law, and the purging of old records.

1. Who is subject to the Public Records Law?

All agencies and officials of the state and local government are required to comply with this law. (See G.S. 132-1.) This, of course, includes districts, supervisors, and state and local soil and water conservation staff. The case law indicates that nonprofit organizations that have close ties to public agencies may be subject to the Public Records Law.

2. What public records are subject to this law?
Just about anything that you have on paper or on tape relating to soil
and water conservation business is a "public record," with a handful
of exceptions. (For exceptions, see Question 4 below.)

The statute lists as public records not only documents and papers
but "maps, books, photographs, films, sound recordings, magnetic or
other tapes, electronic data processing records and artifacts . . . regardless of physical form or characteristics." (See G.S. 132-1.) There is no
clear statement in the statute or in the North Carolina case law as to
whether rough notes kept by a public employee are public records.
Some courts in states other than North Carolina have held that such
notes are public records, and some courts have held otherwise. (See
Lawrence, *Public Records*, pages 9 through 11.)

*3. What are the duties of a district or state employee or official under
the Public Records Law?*
We start from the provision of the law that any public record can "be
inspected and examined at reasonable times and under reasonable supervision by any person." (See G.S. 132-6.) Thus, every district or state
employee or official having custody of public records must permit them
to be examined at reasonable times by any person. Without getting lost in
details, here are a few points to remember about this basic requirement:

- There is no limit in the statute on the "persons," natural or arti-
  ficial, who have the right of inspection. They all do.
- In addition to the right of inspection, the citizen is entitled to a
  copy of the record (certified or uncertified, at the citizen's
  option), which must be provided by the custodian. (See G.S.
  132-6, 132-6.2.)
- A fee may be charged for copying, but not for inspection. The
  amount of the copying fee is limited by G.S. 132-6.2 to "actual
  costs"—"direct, chargeable costs related to reproduction . . . as
  determined by general accounting principles." Nominal charges
  probably don't have to be supported by accounting principles.
- The motive of the citizen to inspect and copy, whether commercial or to monitor government operations, is irrelevant. You
  can't question their motives. [See G.S. 136-6(b) and Lawrence,
  Public Records, pages 30 and 31.]

- The statute does not define the requirement to allow inspection at "reasonable times." A commonsense interpretation would be during regular office hours of the custodian. If there are no regular office hours, the custodian probably still must provide some opportunity for inspection and copying. (See Lawrence, *Public Records*, pages 34 and 35.)

The statute does not say how quickly the custodian must respond to a request. Courts would probably judge this by a standard of "reasonableness." A prompt response to a simple request is indicated. More time would be reasonable for more complex requests, especially if the custodian requires time to locate and deliver records. (See Lawrence, *Public Records*, pages 36 and 37.)

Sometimes citizens will ask for public records by telephone. The statute does not require the custodian to respond to a telephone request, but in practice many custodians do respond. (See Lawrence, *Public Records*, page 40.)

In general, the statute does not require custodians to create new records that don't exist, as by compiling information from their records. [See G.S. 132-6.2(c).] There is one exception to this rule: G.S. 132-6.1(b) requires that each public agency that creates a computer database (after July 1, 1998, for districts) must create an index for the database.

You may combine public and confidential records, but this does not excuse you from allowing access to the public portion of the records. The usual solution is for you either to extract the public portions or excise the confidential portions. (See Lawrence, *Public Records*, pages 19 and 20.)

If a district office has federal records in its files, such as NRCS information, the district is probably obligated to allow inspection and copying of this federal information unless a federal statute or rule expressly prohibits this. (For example, in a lawsuit over a hog lot, one district office was subpoenaed to produce all of its personnel files on the hog farms, including NRCS data in the file.) If it is important to restrict public access to information gathered by NRCS from landowners, it may be a solution to separate out NRCS records and keep them in NRCS files.

4. You mentioned "exceptions." What are the exceptions from the obligation to allow inspection?

There are a few statutory exceptions to the Public Records Law, including the following.

PERSONNEL. There is a limited exemption of personnel records of county employees that allows citizens to inspect personnel files for information concerning the following subjects and only these subjects: an employee's name, age, date of original appointment, current position title, current salary, date and amount of most recent salary increase or decrease, date of most recent classification change, and current office. (See G.S. 153A-98 and Lawrence, *Public Records*, page 84.) If the district board wants to treat "county employees" and those who are technically "district employees" consistently, the board may wish to adopt a resolution that accomplishes this. (See Lawrence, *Public Records*, pages 86 through 88.)

SOCIAL SECURITY NUMBERS. Federal law prohibits disclosure of Social Security account numbers unless required by a statute, regulation, or ordinance adopted before October 1, 1990. [See 42 USC § 405(c)(2)(C)(viii).] Also, federal law limits the use of account numbers submitted for a welfare program to that program. State law does not allow public access to account numbers collected from employees, social services clients, or patients at a health care facility. (See Lawrence, *Public Records*, pages 202 and 203.) In all other respects, Social Security account numbers in the possession of local governments (such as districts) are subject to the Public Records Law.

ATTORNEY-CLIENT COMMUNICATIONS. Written communications from the district's attorney that involve a claim (by or against the district), a lawsuit, or an administrative proceeding are not subject to mandatory inspection. G.S. 132-1.1(a) provides that these communications become public records, however, three years after the board receives them. It is possible that there is a broader attorney "work product" exception from inspection, but the case law on this subject is unclear. (See Lawrence, *Public Records*, page 126.)

SETTLEMENTS. Settlement documents in lawsuits, administrative proceedings, or arbitrations against a governmental unit are not exempt unless they involve a medical malpractice suit against a hospital, or the settlement is sealed by a court or administrative tribunal. The sealed-document exception is limited to situations where the court order spells out the rationale for overcoming a presumption in favor of openness. (See G.S. 132-1.3, and Lawrence, *Public Records*, pages 142 and 143.)

TRADE SECRETS. Business interests often want their trade secrets to be kept private. There is a Public Records Law exception that denies access to those trade secrets that are owned by private persons and designated by them as confidential or a trade secret when the information is first furnished to a public agency. This exception is only available to a person who is performing under or bidding on a public contact; applying for a permit or for participation in a government program; responding to a governmental request for proposals (RFP); undertaking an industrial development project; or demonstrating compliance with law. (See G.S. 132-1.2; Lawrence, *Public Records*, page 132.)

CRIMINAL INVESTIGATIONS. There is an exception for records of criminal investigations and compilations of criminal intelligence information. (See G.S. 132-1.4.) This exception obviously is aimed primarily at records maintained by law enforcement agencies. If a question arises about information concerning criminal violations contained in a district's files, the district should consult an attorney before acting on a request for access to that information.

LOCAL TAX RECORDS. Two statutes prohibit release of local tax records that contain information about a taxpayer's income or receipts. (See G.S. 160A-208.1 and 153A-148.1.) A violation of either of these statutes is a Class 1 misdemeanor and violators are to be dismissed from office and banned from public office or employment for five years. Local taxes measured by receipts are most likely to generate this information. (See Lawrence, *Public Records*, pages 150 and 151.) It may be unlikely that district files will contain the records targeted by these statutes, but a district that has questions about this issue might contact David Lawrence at the Institute of Government for advice.

CONTRACT BID DOCUMENTS. G.S. 133-53 allows state and local governments to exclude from public access cost estimates for a project and lists of contractors who have obtained proposals for bid purposes. The agency must adopt a regulation to exclude the matter from public access. (See Lawrence, *Public Records*, page 188.)

GEOGRAPHICAL INFORMATION SYSTEMS. The Public Records Law requires local governments to provide public access to geographical information systems (GIS) and to provide copies of GIS records at

reasonable cost. However, G.S. 132-10 does allow local governments
to deny electronic copies of a GIS database to anyone who refuses to
enter a written contract in which they agree *not* to use the copies for
trade or commercial purposes. (This statute literally applies only to
"counties and cities." A district that has a GIS database may want to
consult with its attorney or the Attorney General's office or David
Lawrence concerning the application of the statute to districts.)

MISCELLANEOUS. Other statutory provisions concerning access to
medical and patient records and access to records of government
loan programs and public enterprises seem unlikely to be of concern
for districts.

5. What procedures should you follow to purge old district records?
G.S. 132-3 prohibits any public official from destroying, selling, lend-
ing or otherwise disposing of a public record except in accordance
with procedures set forth in G.S. 121-5 without the consent of the
N.C. Department of Cultural Resources. That section empowers the
department to decide how long particular categories of records are
kept and whether they may be destroyed. The department has adopted
a series of records retention and disposal schedules.

The district board needs to agree to a schedule for disposal of
records. Methods allowed for disposal of records include burning,
shredding, acid reduction, burying, and selling the records as waste
paper under an agreement by the purchaser not to resell them as documents or records. These are the only methods that the law allows for
records disposal. (See Lawrence, *Public Records*, pages 51 and 52.)

A district that has not already made routine arrangements with the
Department of Cultural Resources for records purging can call the
Division of Archives and Records for advice on the proper procedure
at (919) 733-3540.

*6. What other responsibility does the district have for records
management?*
G.S. 132-2 makes the person in charge of a district office the custodian
of its public records. G.S. Chapter 132 also imposes on the custodian
the responsibility to maintain and preserve the public records; to repair
or renovate worn or damaged records; to bring suit to recover records;
to bring suit to recover records held improperly by others; to permit

public inspection and provide copies of records; and to deliver the records to his or her successor. (See Lawrence, *Public Records*, pages 48 through 50.)

7. What are the consequences of failing to abide by the provisions of the Public Records Law?

G.S. 132-9 gives to any person denied rightful access to public records the right to bring suit in the General Court of Justice to redress these grievances. The suit is to be set down for immediate hearing and the court may award reasonable attorney fees to the prevailing party— even against an employee or official who knowingly and intentionally violated the law.

G.S. 132-3(a) prohibits a public official from disposing of a public record without the consent of the Department of Cultural Resources. This section declares it to be a Class 3 misdemeanor (punishable by a fine of $10 to $500) to destroy or alter a public record or to unlawfully remove it from the office where it is usually kept. G.S. 132-4 makes it a Class 1 misdemeanor for the custodian of public records to fail to deliver them, at the expiration of the custodian's term, to the person authorized to receive them.

Conclusion

Both the open meetings and public records laws impose important responsibilities on the districts, the State Division, and the State Commission. Those responsibilities are not static because the General Assembly frequently amends these laws. At the district level it would be good practice, not only for a staff member to be knowledgeable about these laws but for at least one district supervisor to be knowledgeable also. The districts should feel free to consult with David Lawrence, the Institute's expert on these laws, for advice and suggestions, or with the Attorney General's office. If you need more information on the public records law, you can buy a detailed guide from the Institute of Government (David M. Lawrence, *Public Records Law for North Carolina Local Governments,* 1997, and *1997–1998 Supplement*).

8
District Finance

Milton S. Heath, Jr.

The Local Government Budget and Fiscal Control Act has been on the statute books of North Carolina since 1971. It is a comprehensive law for all local government budgets, audits, and fiscal controls, but it allows enough flexibility for local governments (including soil and water conservation districts) to select procedures that reasonably fit their needs.

Experienced district supervisors can recall when the districts were not familiar with the provisions of this statute and—needless to say—did not follow its procedures. Beginning in the late 1980s, however, the districts were helped to come under the act by the Local Government Commission. The districts by now have made the choices and taken the steps necessary to come into compliance with this law. They have come to recognize it as one of those statutes that the districts are obligated to follow.

This chapter summarizes the principal requirements of the Budget and Fiscal Control Act for districts under three headings: applicability, budgeting, and audits and other fiscal controls. Every district office should keep a copy of the act for district supervisors and staff to consult. The act is also available on the Internet.

Applicability of the Act (Question 1)

1. What makes the Budget and Fiscal Control Act applicable to soil and water conservation districts?
Section 159-7(c) of the North Carolina General Statutes (hereinafter G.S.) states that "It is the intent of the General Assembly by enactment

---

Milton S. Heath, Jr., joined the Institute of Government faculty in 1957 and has specialized in conservation and environmental law and programs for over forty-five years.

of this Article to prescribe for local governments and public authorities
a uniform system of budget adoption and administration and fiscal
control." The same section defines a "public authority" broadly
enough to include soil and water conservation districts, stating that a
public authority, under G.S. 159-7(b), is a "municipal corporation . . .
that is not subject to the [state] Executive Budget Act."

Several parts of the Act, especially G.S. 159-7(b)(10) and (15), give
districts the choice of coming under the county's budgets or audits, or
of doing their own budgets or audits. In either case, the act's procedures apply.

Budgets

The Basic Budgeting Requirements of the Act (Questions 2 and 3)
2. *What are the basic requirements of the Budget and Fiscal
Control Act?*
The basic budgeting requirements are

- A balanced budget
- An annual budget process, including a budget ordinance
- A budget officer
- Inclusiveness

A few comments on each requirement follow. District supervisors
are encouraged to examine the act on their own for details that are not
covered in this brief summary of the basics.

A BALANCED BUDGET (G.S. 159-8). North Carolina local governments must operate under an annual balanced budget, that is, the sum
of estimated net revenues and appropriated fund balances must be
equal to appropriations. Conservative management would aim at
maintaining a small leftover fund balance.

ANNUAL BUDGET PROCESS (G.S. 159-11 to 12). The act spells out
the annual budget process, including the following key steps and dates:

- Before April 30, departments must submit their budget requests
  and revenue estimates to the budget officer in the form set by the
  budget officer.
- By June 1 the budget officer must submit the budget and budget
  message to the governing board, preferably at a formal meeting.
  The board must hold a public hearing on the budget.

- The budget officer must file a copy with the clerk to the board on the day the budget is submitted to the board, to be open for public inspection. The clerk must make copies available to all news media in the county and publish a statement of the budget's availability with notice of the place and time of the hearing.
- Not earlier than ten days after the budget is submitted by the budget officer and not later than July 1, the board must adopt the budget ordinance.

BUDGET OFFICER (G.S. 159-9). Each local government and public authority must appoint a budget officer to serve at the will of the governing board. In cities and counties, the city or county manager is ex officio budget officer. In other local governments and in public authorities, the duties of the budget officer may be imposed on the chair or a member of the governing board or any other officer or employee.

THE BUDGET ORDINANCE (G.S. 159-13, 15, 16). G.S. 159-13 spells out detailed requirements for the budget ordinance. The basic requirements are that it must be balanced and must make appropriations by department, function, or project, and show revenues by major source. The ordinance must be entered in the board's minutes and copies must be filed with the finance officer, the budget officer, and the clerk to the board. The ordinance can be amended at any time after adoption. If adoption of the budget is delayed beyond July 1, the board shall make interim appropriations to pay salaries and usual ordinary expenses, and to pay debt service until the ordinance is adopted.

PROJECT ORDINANCES (G.S. 159-13.2). G.S. 159-13.2 allows adoption of project ordinances for acquisition of capital assets or for grant-financed projects. A project ordinance must be balanced over the life of the project. It can be adopted at any time, and it need not be re-adopted in a subsequent fiscal year. Spending authority extends for the life of the project; unused spending authority carries over beyond June 30. A project ordinance may be amended as needed during a project's life, so long as it remains in balance. The usual filing and minutes requirements apply.

The project ordinance procedure allows some flexibility for districts and other local governments for grants and capital acquisitions that do not fit well into the annual budget procedure.

THE REQUIREMENT OF INCLUSIVENESS. A basic requirement of the Budget and Fiscal Control Act is inclusiveness: all district moneys must be budgeted before being spent. G.S. 159-8(a) states that no "local government or public authority may expend any moneys, regardless of their sources . . . except in accordance with a budget ordinance or project ordinance . . . or through an intragovernmental service fund or trust and agency fund."

3. What Budgeting Options Are Available to Districts?
The districts have two basic budgeting options: they can come under the budgets of their county governments or they can enact and manage their own budgets. Over the years a majority of the districts have found it more desirable or convenient to come under the county budget, but some districts continue to manage their own budgets.

The districts that come under the county budget must file their budget requests with the county budget officer before April 30—most of them file sooner. After April 30, the county is responsible for the budget process in accordance with the Budget and Fiscal Control Act. These districts may gain better access to the county's financial resources than the districts that have their own budgets. In order to protect the districts' interests, of course, their supervisors will need to monitor the county budget process and stay in touch with their county commissioners.

The districts that choose to enact and manage their own budgets must meet all of the budgeting requirements of the Budget and Fiscal Control Act, which can be demanding. The independence that they gain is not without its price.

Financial Administration and Fiscal Controls

The Finance Officer and the Fiscal Control Requirements. (Questions 4 and 5)
4. What are the Act's requirements for financial administration?
FINANCE OFFICER. If a district manages its own affairs, G.S. 159-24 requires the District Board to appoint a finance officer to serve at its pleasure. The finance officer may be a district staff member, a board member, or the district's budget officer.

The title of this office may be treasurer, accountant, finance director, finance officer, or any other reasonably descriptive title. G.S. 159-25 spells out the finance officer's duties, which include keeping accounts, disbursing funds, preparing statements of financial condition, maintaining records of district obligations, and supervising idle funds.

If the county manages the district's affairs, the county finance officer is responsible for the financial administration of the district.

5. What are the act's fiscal control requirements?
PRE-AUDIT. G.S. 159-28 spells out the pre-audit requirements of the act. Under these requirements the finance officer must

- Review every contract, purchase order, or other obligation to determine if it is covered by an appropriation in the budget ordinance or a project ordinance and if there is a balance in the appropriation to pay it.
- Stamp any contract or purchase order with a certificate stating that it has been pre-audited as required by the act.
- Certify that every check or draft on an official depository has been approved as required by the act. (There is a procedure that allows the board to approve a bill or invoice that has been disapproved by the finance officer.)
- Sign and disburse any check or draft for the payment of district funds.

If the county manages the district's fiscal affairs, the county finance officer or board of commissioners may be willing to deputize a district official to perform pre-audit functions and payment authorization and disbursement duties.

BANK ACCOUNTS. The governing body of any local government selects the unit's own official depositories (banks, savings and loans, or trust companies), and the funds can be deposited only in an official depository. (See G.S. 159-31.) If the county is managing a district's affairs, the district cannot have its own bank account unless the county commissioners authorize it. This is a subject that might be addressed by the district-county operational agreement. (See Chapter 14.)

DAILY DEPOSIT. The daily deposit law, G.S. 159-32, governs deposits of all moneys collected or received by local government employees or officials. It requires each officer and employee to deposit collections and receipts daily with the finance officer or in an official depository. This requires one deposit per day. The governing board, however, may authorize daily deposits only when $250 or more is on hand, except that a deposit shall be made on the last business day of the month.

ANNUAL INDEPENDENT AUDIT. G.S. 159-34 requires each local government to have an annual independent audit, to be performed in conformity with generally accepted accounting principles and auditing standards. The audit contract must be approved by staff to the Local Government Commission, and the completed audit must be filed with the secretary of the Local Government Commission. An audit is a complex and expensive process. If the district's affairs are managed by the county, the annual audit of the county covers the district.

G.S. 139-7 allows the district that manages its own affairs a simpler alternative, that is, to provide in any year an "internal audit." The chair of the board is required to certify under oath that the internal audit is a true and accurate reflection of the accounts and disbursements, which puts the chair on the line for the district's audit. A district that chooses to go this route might wish to create an audit committee to assist the chair.

G.S. 139-7 also requires the supervisors to provide for the execution of security bonds for all officers and employees who are entrusted with money or property.

9

District Personnel Management and Administration

Milton S. Heath, Jr.

The Changing Picture of Local Soil and Water Conservation Staffing

In the early years of soil and water conservation in North Carolina, a typical district might have a part-time secretary on loan from the county and a district conservationist, who was trained and employed by the U.S. Soil Conservation Service. Today, the typical district office of the early twenty-first century may have anywhere from two to eleven employees, depending on the county. These employees have a broad range of skills, training, and titles, and their appointments are likely to be a mixture of district, county, and federal.

Some Basic Questions about Local Soil and Water Conservation Staffs

A new district supervisor who visits the local district office could be expected to ask who hires, fires, supervises, and sets the pay levels of the local employees in the office. If the supervisor assumes that the district board does all of these things, he or she might be in for a surprise. This chapter addresses these questions and points the new supervisor in the direction of some answers.

A major purpose of this chapter is to make district supervisors aware of the North Carolina statutes that govern the hiring, firing, and

Milton S. Heath, Jr., joined the Institute of Government faculty in 1957 and has specialized in conservation and environmental law and programs for over forty-five years.

supervision of local soil and water conservation employees, and their compensation.

It is also important for the supervisors to know that some of the local employees in the district office are "county" employees and others may be "district" (but not county) employees. This distinction may have important consequences for hiring, firing, supervision, and compensation. Moreover, it may not always be easy to tell whether a particular local employee is district or county.

The main topics in this chapter are

- North Carolina statutory provisions concerning hiring, firing, supervising, and compensating local soil and water conservation employees
- Some personnel implications of being a district employee or a county employee
- The district-county operational agreement
- Staffing patterns of North Carolina districts
- Basic questions

Basic Statutory Provisions, Personnel Implications, and Operational Agreements (Questions 1 through 3)

1. What are the basic statutory provisions concerning hiring and firing of local soil and water conservation staff?
The state soil and water conservation district law empowers the district supervisors to hire secretaries and other employees. [See Section 139-7 of the North Carolina General Statutes (hereinafter G.S.)] It says nothing directly about the power to fire employees, but it has been assumed that the supervisors may fire those whom they hired, unless some other statute provides otherwise. Nor does the statute say who has the authority to supervise district staff.

Two other statutes might put the hiring and firing of local soil and water conservation staff in different hands, if the local staff were treated as county employees rather than district employees. (Districts may want them to be treated as county employees in order for them to be eligible for county personnel benefits.)

G.S. 153A-82 (part of North Carolina's county law) authorizes the county manager in a manager county (with the approval of the county commissioners) to appoint and remove county employees. G.S. 153A-

87 authorizes the board of commissioners in non-manager counties to appoint and remove county employees. Neither of these statutes says anything directly about the supervision of county employees.

Neither the soil and water conservation law nor the county law gives any guidance about who is to make the decision as to whether local soil and water conservation staff are to be hired by the district supervisors or by the county manager or county commissioners. Is this affected by who pays the local soil and water conservation staff? The statutes do not speak to this question either.

This seems to leave room for an enterprising district board to decide whether to do the hiring itself or to ask the county to do the hiring independently or upon the recommendation of the district.

The flexibility that these statutes create places a premium on careful record-keeping concerning employment decisions, so that future district boards can accurately determine who made hiring and firing decisions and what procedures were used. This flexibility also creates an incentive to use the district-county operational agreement to address these issues. (See Chapter 14.)

It is important for the county and the district to have clear and consistent understandings of these matters. For example, if the district board believes that it hired a particular employee independently as a district employee, but the county manager believes that the district was delegated the authority to hire this person as a county employee, this can be a source of serious disagreement when it becomes necessary to discipline or fire the employee.

2. What are the personnel implications of being a district employee or a county employee?
If the local employees are hired by the county managers, the county managers can suspend or fire them. (See G.S. 153A-82.)

If the local employees are hired by the county commissioners, the county commissioners can suspend or fire them. (See G.S. 153A-87.)

The board of county commissioners sets or approves compensation schedules for all county employees. ("County employees" would include all local soil and water conservation employees in a county department, as well as those who were hired by the county manager or county commissioners.) (See G.S. 153A-82.)

In a county manager county, the county manager directs and supervises the administration of all county departments and of all county boards under the general control of the county commissioners. The county manager also sees that all orders, ordinances, resolutions, and regulations of the county commissioners are faithfully executed. (See G.S. 153A-82.)

If the county's employment policies have been incorporated in a commissioners' order, ordinance, resolution, or regulation, those policies probably cover all local soil and water conservation employees hired by the county, and possibly those paid from county funds but not hired by the county.

If local employees are hired and paid by the district, the supervisors probably have exclusive authority to fire or discipline the employees, and to supervise them. The supervisors could probably apply the district's employment policies to them (G.S. 139-7).

If local employees are hired by the district but paid by the county, we are in a gray area, which might be clarified in the district-county operational agreement. (See Chapter 14.)

The county has the legal authority to defend local soil and water conservation personnel who are county employees or district employees or district supervisors against civil or criminal actions and to pay judgments against them, under G.S. 153A-98 and 160A-167. (The employee or supervisor must request the defense and payment in a timely fashion in order to preserve these rights.) At one time, the law was not clear on whether district supervisors were entitled to these rights. These doubts were cleared up by legislation amending these statutes in 2001.

3. How can the district supervisors address personnel issues through the district-county operational agreement and the cooperative working agreement?

Chapter 14 of this *Guidebook* examines more fully three basic agreements that support the conservation partnership: the mutual agreement, the cooperative working agreement, and the operational agreement.

The mutual agreement describes the relationship between the local district, the U.S. Department of Agriculture, and the state of North Carolina.

The operational agreement describes the day-to-day working relationship between the districts, the NRCS, the North Carolina Division of Soil and Water Conservation, and the local county government. It is signed by representatives of all four parties and can be amended at any time with the concurrence of all of the parties. In many districts it is reviewed at least annually; among other things, it can be used to clarify or resolve district-county personnel issues. The area coordinator who serves any district can help the district board learn how other districts have used the operational agreement in this way.

The cooperative working agreement is a useful source of information about administrative and technical supervision and oversight responsibilities. Every district supervisor should become familiar with this agreement as well as the other two basic agreements.

Current District Staffing Patterns and Basic Questions for District Supervisors (Questions 4 and 5)

4. What are the current staffing patterns of North Carolina districts? About three-fourths of the local soil and water conservation districts have local offices with one or more staff members employed by the county and one or more staff members who are federal (NRCS) employees working part-time or full-time out of those offices.

About one-fifth of the districts have one or more staff members employed by the district, plus one or more NRCS employees working part-time or full-time.

Six districts have NRCS staff, plus some local staff employed by the county and some employed by the district.[1]

Staff size in the districts ranges from one person in Dare to eleven in Duplin. Over two-thirds of the districts have either three or four staff members.

A typical three-person district staff consists of

- The district conservationist, a federal employee of NRCS
- Two county employees—an office manager, secretary, or administrator and a district or cost-share technician

If there is a fourth employee in the district, it will most commonly be a soil conservationist or soils technician. Districts with five or more staff members may have additional technicians or conservationists. Some of the districts also have engineers, natural resource conservationists, environmental specialists, conservation specialists, education

---

1. Note that the 1999 directory indicates whether local employees are employed by the county or by the district. The 2003 directory does not make this distinction.

specialists, river basin or watershed conservationists, stream bank technicians, animal operation specialists, waste management or water quality specialists, computer or data specialists, or associate supervisors.

These different hiring patterns may mean that there are different answers from one district to another for questions such as

- Who hires, fires and disciplines local staff?
- Who supervises local staff?
- Who sets pay scales and employment policies for local staff?

5. What basic questions might a district board ask about its local staff? Figure 9-1 provides a set of fundamental employment questions that any district board might want to consider from time to time. It would not be surprising if the answers varied from district to district, and even within a single district.

Figure 9-1. Basic employment questions for district boards to consider

1. Who hires local soil and water conservation employees?

    A. District board of supervisors?
    B. Board of county commissioners?
    C. County manager?
    D. All of the above?
    Who in fact hired the present local employees?

2. Who can fire a local soil and water conservation employee?

    A. District board of supervisors?
    B. The appointing official or board?

3. Who supervises local soil and water conservation employees?

    A. District board of supervisors?
    B. NRCS district conservationist?
    C. County manager?
    D. Board of county commissioners?
    E. It varies from district to district?

4. Who sets pay levels for local soil and water conservation employees

    A. District board of supervisors?
    B. County manager?
    C. Board of county commissioners?
    D. It varies from district to district and by type of employee?

5. Who really decides or should decide on these hiring, firing, supervision, and compensation questions?

(continued on page 94)

Figure 9-1. Basic employment questions for district boards to consider (*continued*)

6. What ought to be the basis for these decisions?

   A district secretary was hired by the district board but is paid by the county.

   The district secretary allegedly said something that violates a county or federal policy, or is suspected of taking a small amount of money from the petty cash fund.

   The county manager tells the district board that the manager is responsible for firing or otherwise disciplining all employees paid by the county.

   Can (or should) the district board hold the line on right-to-fire or discipline a secretary appointed by the district, or should the district board agree with the county manager?

   Answers to "Basic Questions" above:
   1. D
   2. B
   3. E
   4. D
   5. and 6. Each district must find its own answers.

10

The North Carolina Conservation District Employees' Association

Gail M. Hughes

1. How was the District Employees' Association formed?
The idea of a state conservation district employees association began
in 1989 when an inquiry about a national association was received.
Employees decided to get involved with a state association as well as a
southeast and national association.

The initial contact with each district employee in Area 1 was made by
phone; and because of the interest shown by employees, a meeting was
held to discuss an association. On August 24, 1989, at the Buncombe
Soil and Water Conservation District office, twelve employees representing six districts met and discussed goals for an association. From that
meeting an ad hoc committee consisting of five employees from Area 1
was formed. Those serving on the committee were Martha Buff, Bob
Cathey, Marlene Harrell, Gary Higgins, and Janet Nichols.

A survey and minutes from the meeting were distributed throughout
the state. With the survey results in favor of an association, the ad hoc
committee met again on September 21, 1989, to discuss draft bylaws
and next steps. On October 26, 1989, Area 1 supervisors voted to accept
a resolution submitted by the McDowell district in support of a North
Carolina district employees' association.

On January 6, 1990, in Greensboro, North Carolina, during the
North Carolina Association of Soil and Water Conservation Districts
(NCASWCD) meeting, the supervisors voted to support the forming of
a district employees' association. Shortly after this endorsement, the
first session of thirty-two district employees statewide met. Employees

---

Gail M. Hughes is an Orange County District soil conservationist and former
president of the District Employees' Association

present gathered in groups according to their respective areas and selected representatives to serve as members of the steering committee. The steering committee served until the slate of officers was presented at the District Employees Workshop in May 1990.

The steering committee met on January 26, 1990, at the district office building in Greensboro. A discussion was held on goals and expectations of the formation of a District Employees' Association (DEA). Another meeting was held on March 29, 1990, to discuss the upcoming District Employees' Workshop.

On May 24, 1990, at Kill Devil Hills, North Carolina, the employees association was formed and bylaws were reviewed and approved by all members. Martha Buff, McDowell County, served as the first North Carolina DEA president; Millie Langley, Guilford County, first vice president; George Pettus, Wayne County, second vice president; Ginger O'Neal, Perquimans County, secretary; and Fran Murdock, Henderson County, treasurer. The remaining board of directors included: Area 1— Bob Cathey, Henderson County, and alternate Gary Higgins, Buncombe County; Area 2—Brenda R. Parks, Wilkes County, and alternate Nancy Smyre, Catawba County; Area 3—Charlotte Braxton, Chatham County, and alternate Gail Hughes, Orange County; Area 4—Gloria Poythress, Wilson County, and alternate Lillian Hearn, Durham County; Area 5— Nan Laughton, Chowan County, and alternate Wanda Waters, Washington County; Area 6—Mamie Wilson Caison, Brunswick County; Area 7—Laura Simmons, Robeson County; and Area 8—Jim Summers, Iredell County, and alternate Tim Latham, Davie County.

Since the formation of DEA, district employees have been invited to participate in NCASWCD and NRCS committees/special committees and various U.S. Department of Agriculture committees.

DEA needs to continue to work with our district officials at the local, state, regional, and national levels to ensure that districts remain the delivery system for natural resource management programs.

The presidents of DEA are listed in Table 10-1. Presidents have served one-year terms until the current term. The association voted to extend the term to two years, beginning with the incumbent, John Stevenson.

Table 10-1 North Carolina District Employees Association Presidents

1990–1991	Martha Buff	McDowell County
1991–1992	Millie Langley	Guilford County
1992–1993	George Pettus	Wayne County
1993–1994	Bob Cathey	Henderson County
1994–1995	Gail Hughes	Orange County
1995–1996	Nan Laughton	Chowan County
1996–1997	Jim Summers	Iredell County
1997–1998	Phil Ross	Alamance County
1998–1999	Mamie Caison	Brunswick County
1999–2000	Tom Smith	Stokes County
2000–2001	Tommy Brooks	Lee County
2001–2002	Bryan Evans	Pitt County
2002–2004	John Stevenson	Iredell County

2. What are the purposes of DEA?
The basic purposes of DEA, as reflected in its bylaws, are

- To strengthen the local soil and water conservation districts of North Carolina.
- To provide assistance and information to the local boards of supervisors and to the employees of the districts to resolve problems related to renewable natural resource conservation.
- To assist any agency, organization, municipality, group, or individual that supports the soil and water conservation districts of North Carolina in the spirit of cooperation and sound conservation practice and land use.
- To promote, create, and improve efficiency in the operations of the district offices of the counties of the state.
- To provide a vehicle for personal development of district employees and to assist them to better fulfill their responsibilities.

3. What have been DEA's main activities since its creation in 1990?
Workshops and state association meetings. DEA assists with planning
and coordination of a North Carolina Department of Environment
and Natural Resources (DENR)–sponsored District Employee
Workshop that is held each year. This workshop provides information
and training for technical and administrative employees on current
environmental laws, issues, cost-share programs, and administration
changes.

DEA also assists with the annual NCASWCD meeting by providing
clerical assistance and district employee representation during committee meetings. The clerks assist the division staff with taking minutes
and making approved changes to the association's program objectives.
The district employee representatives make recommendations on program issues and how these issues affect the day-to-day activities within
the district offices.

EMPLOYEE AWARDS. The North Carolina Conservation District
Employees Association developed a certification program for employees,
the Professional District Employee Program (PDEP), based on years of
work experience, continuing education, and active involvement in district and association committees and programs. There are six levels of
certification: Standard, Associate Standard, Professional, Master I,
Master II, and Master III. The program goals are to make the positions
of district employees more professional and to make the general public
more aware of their duties and responsibilities. Through this program,
employees of districts are stimulated to augment their education and to
increase their general knowledge. This helps them to become better
qualified by completing course work and other activities that will
enhance the work that is being performed and their pride in their chosen
profession.

SCHOLARSHIP AWARDS. DEA developed a scholarship awards program in 1994 to provide financial assistance for courses at an accred-
ited institution. Three types of scholarships are awarded. Two are for
students and one is for DEA members. The Resource Conservation
Workshop scholarship is awarded to a high school student planning to
study natural resources, environmental sciences, or agriculture. The
student is selected during the resource convention workshop sponsored
by the Division of Soil and Water Conservation and held at N.C. State

University. The children of DEA members are eligible to apply for a student scholarship. The student chosen must plan to study natural resources or an environmental science–related program. The Professional Growth Scholarship is available to DEA members who wish to improve their professional skills within their job categories, either administrative or technical. The scholarship committee accepts applications from employees from June through February 1.

WEB SITE. DEA has developed a Web site for employees and the general public to learn more about the association. The site is a source of information also for district employees of other states and regions, district supervisors, and the general public. Keeping supervisors and the public informed helps keep employers and clients informed. The site provides an outlet for employees to contact persons from their respective areas of the state and access association information on bylaws, membership, and scholarships, including applications. As DEA is considered a partner in the conservation of natural resources, the site provides links to other conservation and environmental agencies on the Web. The most popular page is "What's Happening," where employees can find the latest information on upcoming meetings or workshops and what's happening on the regional or national level.

TECHNICAL DEVELOPMENT, TRAINING, AND MENTORS. A Technical Development Committee was formed to review best management practices (BMPs) and make suggestions to the State Technical Review Committee of new or innovative ideas that can help protect natural resources. DEA holds an advisory position on the State Technical Review Committee, which approves BMPs for the N.C. Agricultural Cost Share Program. The Technical Development Committee provides a structure to assist not only members but also to district employees across the state by carrying their voice to other partners in conservation. DEA has assisted in conducting "training needs" surveys to find out where and what types of training are needed. DEA has developed a list of mentors that is included in the annual district directory. This provides a contact source for employees to call concerning a specific job or function. Recently the name of this committee was changed to the Employee Development Committee. This name change reflects the broader focus of this committee, since DEA serves all employees, both technical and administrative.

OTHER SERVICE. DEA formed a Past President's Association that will assist the board of directors with special projects as needed.

Employees have been asked to be representatives on various USDA–NRCS and NCSWCD association committees. Many employees serve on regional and national employee committees. Former state president Bob Cathey served as the southeast association president, and Martha Buff served as southeast association president and national association president for three years. Currently, past state president Tommy Brooks is the Southeast regional president. David Cash, Area 4 director, is the southeast regional treasurer. Many of the North Carolina District Employees' Association's ideas and programs have been used to help shape programs in other states and on the national level.

11

Liability Issues

Milton S. Heath, Jr.

American public officials everywhere face a risk of civil liability in lawsuits over grievances arising from their governmental activities. Soil and water conservation officials and agencies are no exception.

Fortunately, the number of civil suits that have been brought against North Carolina conservation officials is not large. Enough suits of this kind have been brought or threatened, however, to be a source of concern that justifies a chapter on liability in this *Guidebook*.

Potential Lawsuits (Questions 1 through 5)

1. What soil and water conservation activities might give rise to liability?
RISKS THAT EVERYONE HAS TO LIVE WITH, WHERE THE BEST DEFENSE IS "REASONABLE CARE," OR FOLLOWING THE RULES. In modern society there are some liability-prone situations that everyone must live with, where the best defense is to follow the rules and behave with reasonable care in the circumstances. Among the most obvious examples that may affect conservation agencies and officials are

- Vehicle accidents
- "Slip-and-fall" accidents that may arise in a district office or on field trips

The best advice for district officials here is no different than for any organization: drive safely; obey the traffic laws; develop and publicize procedures and policies that will minimize slip-and-fall accidents (or, think like the manager of a grocery store); and consult your local advisers when problems arise.

Milton S. Heath, Jr., joined the Institute of Government faculty in 1957 and has specialized in conservation and environmental law and programs for over forty-five years.

BREACH OF CONTRACT LAWSUITS. Some district activities inevitably
generate contracts that the contracting parties should view as binding
obligations. Agriculture cost-share agreements and construction and
maintenance contracts for small watershed projects are good examples. If districts fail to live up to these agreements, they can expect to
face the possibility of breach-of-contract suits and should be prepared
to consult their legal advisers when problems arise.

INJURIES ASSOCIATED WITH SMALL WATERSHED OR DRAINAGE ACTIVI-
TIES. One of the inevitable risks for districts that sponsor small watershed or drainage projects is that visitors who are invited or allowed to
hike, fish, swim, or engage in other recreational activities may be
injured and will seek compensation from the district for their injuries.
If this happens, the district should promptly contact its attorneys for
assistance.

The body of common law that sets forth the rules of liability for
these situations is known as landowner (or land occupier or premises)
liability. Early common law decisions imposed a legal duty on
landowners to take "reasonable care" to protect business visitors
("invitees") from being injured while on the landowner's property.
The landowner only owed a legal duty not to intentionally injure non-
business visitors, including trespassers and "licensees" (persons on the
property by express or implied permission but not on mutual business). For more than two decades there has been a trend in common-
law decisions to liberalize liability by applying the reasonable care
standard to all entrants or at least to licensees as well as invitees.
About half of the nation's state courts have joined this trend, including
North Carolina in 1998.[1]

In a parallel development, more than forty states have enacted
statutes that protect rural landowners from liability to people who are
injured while hunting, fishing, hiking, swimming, or otherwise using
their land for recreation without charge. These statutes allow rural
landowners to defend liability suits by proving that they did not intentionally injure the people who entered their land without charge. In
1995 North Carolina enacted such a statute, Chapter 38A of the
North Carolina General Statutes (hereinafter G.S.), which protects

1. Nelson v. Freeland, 349 N.C. 615, 507 S.EW.2d 882, applying the reasonable
care standard to licensees. See Dan B. Dobbs, *The Law of Torts*, §§ 231–241, (West
Group, 2001).

landowners who invite or permit others to use their lands without charge for recreational or educational purposes. The statute probably would protect a private landowner or soil and water conservation district supervisor who helped sponsor a small watershed project and who was sued by an injured recreational or educational user of the project. However, if it happened that the district or a county owned an easement or part of the watershed project property, the district or county could not claim this defense because G.S. Chapter 38A does not apply to governmental landowners.

Small watershed project sponsors tried for several years to get legislation enacted that would fill this gap. In 2001, with crucial help from Representative Arlie Culp (a former Soil Conservation Service district conservationist), the North Carolina General Assembly finally enacted such legislation in S.L. 2001-272 (H 983). The legislation adopts the text of G.S. Chapter 38A as an amendment to G.S. Chapter 139, the statute dealing with soil and water conservation districts. This law essentially gives the same protections to districts, supervisors, and other landowners, and it applies only to land associated with watershed improvement projects.

S.L. 2001-272 adds the following sentence: "This statutory rule modifies the common law of North Carolina concerning landowner liability." This sentence indicates a legislative intent that the new statutory rules—rather than the rules laid down in common-law decisions such as *Nelson v. Freeland*—should govern future liability decisions on this subject.

COMPLAINTS ABOUT REGULATIONS, (SUCH AS REGULATIONS CONCERNING ANIMAL WASTES RESULTING FROM HOG LOTS AND POULTRY FARMS). Soil and water conservation districts are not traditional regulatory agencies with permitting and enforcement powers. In recent years, however, the districts have shown a growing interest in water quality protection and animal waste management. This is reflected, for example, in appointments of some district supervisors to the Environmental Management Commission; in the development of the Agriculture Cost Share Program for non-point source pollution control; in the involvement of the Division of Soil and Water Conservation in supervising annual operations reviews of animal operations by technical specialists; and in the designation of several counties for experimental comparison of operations review with counties where animal wastes are regulated in more traditional ways.

None of these activities necessarily draws districts directly into the
regulatory process or into litigation, but these activities make district
supervisors and employees players in the regulatory process in ways
that are novel to the traditional conservation movement. If these activities give some district supervisors and employees an opportunity to
influence the regulatory process, they also may expose the same supervisors and employees to some criticism by other supervisors and by
some farmers affected by regulation.

Some farmers and supervisors have suggested that animal waste
regulations constitute a "taking" of their property, but no North
Carolina cases have supported their complaints.

COMPLAINTS ABOUT UNFAIRNESS IN DISTRIBUTING BENEFITS, SUCH
AS COST-SHARE BENEFITS. District supervisors who take part in decisions by the district board on such matters as distribution of cost-share
benefits, or personnel decisions against a local employee should be
careful to avoid prejudging issues that come before them. They should
come to their decisions with unbiased minds.

The leading North Carolina Supreme Court decision on this subject
affirmed a damage award against a local school board that had dismissed a driver education public school teacher, because the bias of
one board member against the teacher had influenced the board's
action.[2] The court adopted a "single member bias rule," that is, the
bias of a single board member tainted the entire decision-making
process. Although the decision directly affected only a quasi-judicial
decision of a board, it should serve as a warning to all board members
about the dangers of allowing their biases to affect their votes in board
decisions.

District supervisors who believe that their personal biases might affect
their votes as board members should ask to be excused from voting.

Another fairness issue involves distribution by board action to individual board members of cost-share and other benefits. Under G.S. 14-
234 it is a misdemeanor for a public official to participate in the award
of a public contract that will benefit him or her individually. In order
to clarify the legal status of payments of agriculture cost-share funds to
district supervisors, the General Assembly in 1995 amended G.S. 14-
234 to add payments of cost-share benefits to district supervisors or

2. Crump v. Board of Education of the Hickory School Administrative Unit,
326 N.C. 603, 392 S.E. 2d 579 (1990).

members of the North Carolina Soil and Water Conservation
Commission (State Commission) to a long list of exceptions to G.S.
14-234. District supervisors and State Commission members may
apply for and receive these grants if they do not vote on the grant
application, do not attempt to influence the board's decision, and the
application of a district supervisor is approved by the State
Commission or the application of a State Commission member is
approved by the secretary of the N.C. Department of Environment and
Natural Resources (DENR).

*2. What kinds of lawsuits may be brought against districts and conser-
vation officials?*
There are many different kinds of lawsuits that might be brought
against districts and conservation officials, but the most prominent
examples in recent experience have been tort actions, contract actions,
and suits brought under federal laws.

TORT ACTIONS are the broad group of damage actions resulting
from personal injuries and property damage. Torts include suits for
negligence, nuisance, civil assault, trespass, defamation (libel and slan-
der), and the like. The very large negligence category may include, for
example, not only suits arising from vehicle accidents and slip-and-fall
accidents but also suits that focus on the failure of district personnel to
abide by rules and regulations that set standards of conduct.

BREACH OF CONTRACT SUITS involving such documents as agriculture cost-share agreements and small watershed construction and
maintenance contracts are good examples of contract suits.

Recent experiences in two southwestern North Carolina counties
illustrate the potential for *litigation in federal courts over federal law
violations.*

After an NRCS employee was convicted in federal court of approving payments to individuals by NRCS, knowing they were false, a suit
was brought in federal district court against a number of defendants.
The suit charged violations of the Federal False Claims Act. It involved
false claims under various federal programs and the North Carolina
Agriculture Cost Share Program.[3]

3. U.S. *ex rel* Karen Wilson v. Cherokee and Graham Soil and Water
Conservation Districts et. al. (U.S. District Court, Western District of N.C., 2000,
Civil Action No. 2:01 CV19T.)

Defendants in this lawsuit included district supervisors and county commissioners from two counties, NRCS and local district employees, and private citizens. The suit charged essentially that all of the defendants collaborated in a scheme or schemes to defraud the federal government. The litigation also involved harassment and retaliation charges brought by a local district employee, the "whistle blower" in this case, who was suing to recover penalties and damages under federal law as a *qui tam* plaintiff who may be entitled to share in a recovery with the federal government. Because of the large number of defendants, county attorneys from both defendant counties, an Assistant Attorney General, and private attorneys were called upon to represent the numerous defendants.

This complex litigation illustrates hitherto unimagined lawsuits arising out of alleged misdeeds of district supervisors, county commissioners, and district and federal employees. It should serve as a warning to district supervisors of the risk of being drawn into expensive and time-consuming litigation if they can plausibly be accused of misusing their offices.

3. Who can be sued?
DISTRICTS. Clearly, districts may be sued, because the District Law expressly authorizes them "to sue and be sued in the name of the district." [See G.S. 139-8(a)(9).]

DISTRICT SUPERVISORS. District supervisors may be sued for actions taken in the course of performing their duties as supervisors. It is very likely that supervisors would be treated as "public officers," since they meet the usual tests applied by the courts to distinguish public officers from public employees. (See Chapter 3, Question 4.) That is, the office of supervisor is created and defined by statute; the supervisors are granted substantial discretionary powers by statute that involve the exercise of sovereign powers; and they take an oath of office. (A reminder to all supervisors—be sure to take the oath! It is a misdemeanor for you to perform official duties without taking the oath. (See G.S. 128-5.)

As public officers, supervisors will be entitled to qualified immunity if they are sued over performance of their duties. The main result of this is that supervisors cannot be held liable for ordinary negligence but only for actions that are corrupt, malicious, or outside the scope of

their duties.)[4] This is an important distinction that protects supervisors
from being second-guessed by the courts for simple negligence in the
performance of their duties.

North Carolina courts have not held individual board members,
such as district supervisors, personally liable for actions taken by their
boards.

DISTRICT EMPLOYEES AND OTHER LOCAL EMPLOYEES. District
employees and other local employees may also be sued over actions
taken in the course of their employment. Unlike district supervisors,
however, district employees are unlikely to be treated by the courts as
public officers. Thus, they probably are not entitled to qualified immunity from suit.[5] They also are probably subject to being sued in their
personal capacity, not merely in their official capacity, and to be personally liable for simple negligence. It is important, therefore, that the
board of supervisors take steps to protect their local employees against
potential liability. (See Question 5, below.)

FEDERAL AND STATE OFFICIALS AND EMPLOYEES. To fill out the picture, federal and state officials and employees are also subject to being
sued over actions taken in the course of their employment. This
includes NRCS personnel and employees of the State Division of Soil
and Water Conservation. The federal defendants would ordinarily be
represented in federal court by federal attorneys and state defendants
by the North Carolina Attorney General. Claims against state personnel ordinarily would be tried under the North Carolina Tort Claims
Act by the North Carolina Industrial Commission.

4. *Where may the defendants be sued: State Court, Federal Court,
Industrial Commission?*
STATE TORT OR CONTRACT SUITS. Traditional tort and contract suits
against districts, supervisors, or local employees would ordinarily be
brought and tried in superior court (that is, in a North Carolina state
court). In some cases the plaintiff may also have the right to seek damages in federal court, or before the North Carolina Industrial
Commission under the State Tort Claims Act.

4. Block v. County of Person, 141 N.C. App. 273, 540 S.E. 2d 415 (N.C. Ct. of
Apps., 2000).
5. *Block v. County of Person*

FEDERAL §1983 SUITS. Damages may also be sought in federal district court under §1983 of the 1871 U.S. Civil Rights Law; §1983 authorizes suits in federal court to recover damages for violating a person's federal constitutional or statutory rights when the violation is caused by the official conduct of a local or state official. It is even possible that separate suits could be filed at the same time in state and federal court if the same conduct that is a state law tort or breach of contract is also a violation of a plaintiff's constitutional or statutory rights. (For example, a civil trespass under state law might also be a violation of a landowner's fourth amendment federal right against an unlawful search or seizure.)

SUITS IN THE INDUSTRIAL COMMISSION. If a negligence suit were brought against a district or supervisor or local employee who was acting as an agent of the state, the suit could be filed in the N.C. Industrial Commission under the State Tort Claims Act, rather than in superior court. The crucial question in such a case is whether a state agency (such as the State Commission or Division of Soil and Water Conservation) exercised such detailed control over the matter in dispute that the local agency (such as a district or district board of supervisors) acted as an agent of the state in dealing with that matter.[6]

5. What can the districts and district supervisors do about liability and the risk of liability?

REPRESENTATION. The first and most important thing for supervisors to do if litigation threatens is to secure capable legal representation. Whatever else you may do, do not go to court or negotiate over a lawsuit without an attorney to represent you. If you are sued or litigation threatens, the supervisors should contact their county attorney and the Attorney General's office. These are the lawyers who clearly have the authority to represent the district, the supervisors, and the local employees.

The District Law entitles the supervisors of a district "to call upon the Attorney General for legal services." (See G.S. 139-7, fourth unnumbered paragraph.) The Attorney General's office has always responded positively to requests from districts for legal assistance,

---

6. Vaughn v. N.C. Department of Human Resources, 296 N.C. 683, 252 S.E. 2d 792 (1979).

including representation in court. For years, the Attorney General has designated at least one Assistant Attorney General to specialize in soil and water conservation law.

The county has the legal authority to represent a district, a supervisor, and any district employee and to pay a judgment against them, but only if you provide notice before a judgment is rendered or a settlement is reached. (See G.S. 153A-97 and 160A-267.) If you are sued, notify the county attorney with copies to the county manager and the chair of the county commissioners immediately. Also notify the Attorney General at the same time. In some cases the county attorney and the Attorney General may decide that you can best be represented by an attorney for the county's insurance company or some other private attorney.

If you receive notice of a deposition in a pending lawsuit, be sure to notify your attorneys. If an attorney for someone who is suing you contacts you, don't give them any more than "name, rank and serial number" and notify your attorneys of the contact.

INSURANCE. Check with your county manager or county finance director as to whether the county's insurance or insurance pool arrangements cover districts, supervisors, and local employees. (Not all counties carry insurance.) Ask the Division of Soil and Water Conservation to keep you current on personal liability coverage available to districts, supervisors, and local soil and water conservation employees.

DEFENSES. There are special defenses to civil suits that may protect supervisors, districts, and local employees. One of these defenses, the "qualified immunity" of district supervisors, has already been mentioned. The districts themselves may be entitled to the defense of sovereign immunity, although this has not been established by North Carolina case law. Your attorney should advise you about the availability of these and other defenses that may protect you in litigation.

OATHS. All district supervisors, both appointed and elected, should take the oath of office. If a supervisor is sued, the taking of the oath will help establish that the supervisor is a public officer entitled to qualified immunity. As already noted, it is a misdemeanor for a supervisor to perform official duties before taking the oath.

THE BOOK. Know the "book" (all of the applicable laws and regulations) and live by the book. It can be devastating to the defense of a lawsuit if it is established on trial that a supervisor or local employee has not abided by your own law, rules, or policies.

BIAS AND UNFAIRNESS. The adverse effects of the bias of any supervisor on any decision of the district board has already been noted. Don't give anyone a basis for accusing any supervisor of bias or unfairness in his or her vote or actions involving district business, such as in distributing benefits or services. A supervisor who knows that he or she is biased against any applicant for cost-share or other benefits should ask the board to be excused from voting, so as to avoid tainting the board's decision.

DOCUMENT, DOCUMENT, DOCUMENT . . . If you are sued or think that you may be sued, be extra careful to document everything that may be pertinent to the suit and not obviously damaging to your counsel. Any experienced litigator will tell you that this may have a decisive effect on your success or failure in the lawsuit.

12

Working with Legislators and County Commissioners

Milton S. Heath, Jr.

District supervisors need to work closely with their legislators and county commissioners because districts are dependent on the General Assembly and their counties for their principal funding and support. All districts were created under legislation enacted by the General Assembly and continue to need legislative support. In short, the health and survival of the districts is linked closely to the counties and the General Assembly.

This chapter is intended to convey some of the important things that the district supervisors need to keep in mind in working with their counties and North Carolina senators and representatives. When you have read this chapter you should have a working understanding of

- The selection and organization of the General Assembly and the board of county commissioners
- The legislative and county commissioner calendars
- Some important legislative and county commissioner deadlines for their constituents (including districts) to keep in mind
- Preparation for legislative sessions by districts and their conservation partners
- Some basic guidelines for working with legislators and county commissioners
- Some food for thought about the strategy of preparing for a legislative session

Milton S. Heath, Jr., joined the Institute of Government faculty in 1957 and has specialized in conservation and environmental law and programs for over forty-five years.

Figure 12-1. Fact Sheet on the Board of County Commissioners

Members, Selection, and Terms

The boards of county commissioners vary in size from three to eleven members, with five members being the typical size. Terms of office may be two or four years, with a trend toward four-year staggered terms. All county commissioners are elected by the people in partisan elections held in November of even-numbered years. Candidates are usually partisan nominees, but this is not required by law.

Chair

In most counties the chair of the board is selected by the board, but in a few counties the chair is elected by the people. The boards that select the chair do so at their first regular meeting in December, for a one-year term. The chair votes on all questions unless excused by rule of the board or by consent of the remaining members.

Meetings

The board of commissioners must meet at least once a month, but they may meet as often as necessary. Many boards have two regular meetings a month. Unless the board votes otherwise, they must meet on the first Monday of each month at the county courthouse.

Ordinances

An ordinance may be adopted at the meeting when it is introduced only by unanimous affirmative vote with all members present and voting. If the ordinance passes this meeting with less than a unanimous vote, it may finally be passed by majority vote at any time within 100 days of its introduction. There are special rules for the budget ordinance, the bond ordinance, a franchise ordinance, and any other ordinance requiring a public hearing.

Budget

The annual budget process for counties set by law requires that the county budget be adopted by July 1. In preparation for that deadline, county departments must submit their budget requests and revenue estimates before April 30, and the budget officer must submit the budget to the commissioners by June 1. Individual counties may set earlier deadlines for departmental requests and submission of the budget. [See Question 2 in Chapter 8 of this *Guidebook*.]

Source: Based on "Counties and County Governance" by Joseph S. Ferrell in County Government in North Carolina, fourth ed., edited by A. Fleming Bell, II, and Warren Jake Wicker (Chapel Hill, N.C.: The University of North Carolina at Chapel Hill, Institute of Government, 1998), chapter 1.

Counties

Some Basic Facts about the Board of Commissioners (Questions 1 through 4)

1. How is the board of county commissioners selected and organized?
County commissioners are elected in November of even-numbered
years for terms that vary from county to county. The size of the boards
varies from three to eleven members. (See Figure 12-1, "Fact Sheet on
the Board of County Commissioners.") District supervisors can ask the
county managers or county boards of elections for the details concerning their counties.

2. When do the county commissioners meet?
The board of county commissioners is required to meet at least once a
month, but may meet more often. Unless the board votes otherwise,
they must meet on the first Monday of each month at the county
courthouse. District supervisors can ask the county managers or clerks
for details. (See Figure 12-1.)

3. What are the key county budget deadlines?
Whether your district manager prepares its own budget or relies on the
county budget, district supervisors need to know the county budget
deadlines by heart. Mark your calendars for these deadlines:

- July 1 for adoption of the county budget;
- June 1 for submission of the proposed budget;
- April 30 for submission of departmental requests (including
  district requests). (See Figure 12-1.)

*4. What recurring problems do districts have in retaining county sup-
port for district programs?*
A recurring problem in some counties is competing with other agencies
and attractions for the attention of the commissioners. Sometimes this
involves overlapping functions; sometimes it does not. District supervisors can only continue to call to the attention of the commissioners
and the manager the services and dollars that soil and water conservation bring to the county. Your regional coordinator may be your best
resource in doing this.

Another recurring problem is the political aspect of the picture for
commissioners, most of whom have to run for office every five years.
Some district supervisors find it easier than others to achieve political
rapport with their commissioners, the best opportunity being election

seasons when both district supervisors and county commissioners are on the ballot at the same time. These days there are always a few former district supervisors (or present appointive supervisors) who serve as county commissioners, which can build a bridge between the two boards.

The General Assembly

Some Basic Facts about the General Assembly (Questions 5 through 9)

For additional information, see Figure 12-2, "Fact Sheet on the General Assembly" and Figure 12-3, "The Legislative Process."

5. How is the General Assembly selected and organized?
North Carolina senators and representatives are elected, in the same elections as the county commissioners, in November of even-numbered years for two-year terms. Early in each biennial legislative session the Speaker of the House and the President Pro Tempore of the Senate appoint standing committees that are staffed by full-time legislative employees. The speaker (who is elected by the House membership) and the Lieutenant Governor (who is elected statewide at the fall elections for a four-year term) preside over the houses.

6. When does the General Assembly meet?
Each General Assembly convenes for a regular session in the odd-numbered years of a biennium (ranging from January 11 to February 9 in recent years). There is no time limit on the length of sessions, which lately have often lasted into late summer or fall. For the last three decades the General Assembly has also convened in late May or early June of the even-numbered years for a session of six weeks or longer, mainly to complete action on the biennial state budget and on bills that passed one house the previous year and were still pending. There also may be extra sessions convened for special purposes (such as redistricting) by the Governor or the presiding officers. And, since the coming of the Governor's veto power, there may be reconvened sessions to consider whether to override vetoes after the General Assembly has adjourned. With all of this near-guaranteed meeting

Figure 12-2. Fact Sheet on the General Assembly

Members	120 House members and 50 senators; elected from separate districts.
Terms	All members serve two-year terms.
Sessions	(1) Regular session in odd-numbered years beginning in January or February and usually lasting through the summer. (No legal limit on length of sessions.) (2) A shorter regular session is usually held in the even-numbered year on budget and other matters. Additional special sessions can be held.
Daily Routines	(1) The full Senate and the House each meet daily, Tuesdays through Thursdays. These meetings usually start early in the afternoon and last from one to three hours. The Senate and House also meet more briefly on Monday nights and Friday mornings. (2) Each Senate and House standing committee usually meets once a week during the sessions at a set morning hour on Tuesday, Wednesday, or Thursday. Some of the busiest committees, such as the Appropriations and Finance committees, meet more often. (3) Senators and Representatives usually get home on weekends where they can be contacted at their homes or offices. Some local delegations caucus at a regular time on Mondays when constituents can meet with them.
Standing Committees	Much of the business of the General Assembly is carried on through standing committees. Ordinarily every bill must be considered by at least one Senate committee and one House committee, and must be favorably reported to the floor in order to be considered by the Senate and House. The speaker appoints committees in the House and the president pro tempore appoints committees in the Senate.
Bills and Laws	For a bill to become law the Senate and House must each pass the same bill, and it must be signed by the Governor. North Carolina was the last state to give its Governor veto power over proposed legislation.

(continued on page 116)

Figure 12-2. Fact Sheet on the General Assembly (*continued*)

Leadership	The presiding officers of the Senate and House are the Lieutenant Governor (Senate) and the speaker (House). They preside over their respective houses and refer bills to committees. Other important leaders include the president pro tem of the Senate, the speaker pro tem of the House, and committee chairmen—especially the chairmen of the Appropriations and Finance committees. The only "legislative leader" who is elected statewide is the Lieutenant Governor.
Staff Lobbyists and State Officials	The staff that serves the General Assembly is becoming more and more important, especially some of the veteran staff members who serve key committees, like the Appropriations Committee, or who represent key leaders like the speaker, Lieutenant Governor, and president pro tempore. Established lobbyists also have an important effect on the results of much legislation, as do the Governor, his cabinet, and members of the Council of State.

time, it is little wonder that people ask whether North Carolina still has a part-time "citizen legislature"!

When the General Assembly is in session, it meets daily, Tuesdays through Thursdays, and usually convenes for a brief evening session on Mondays. Standing committees usually meet once a week on Tuesdays through Thursdays, or more often in the case of the busiest committees, such as appropriations and finance. Committee memberships are announced early in the odd-numbered sessions by the speaker and president pro tempore.

With this busy schedule, the best opportunities for constituents, such as district supervisors, to meet with their legislators during sessions is at home over the weekends. Some legislative delegations hold caucuses to meet constituents at regular times on Mondays or on a weekend day.

7. What important deadlines are there during legislative sessions?
Every session the General Assembly will set a series of deadlines designed to manage the business of the session and keep it moving.

Figure 12-3. Major Steps in the Legislative Process

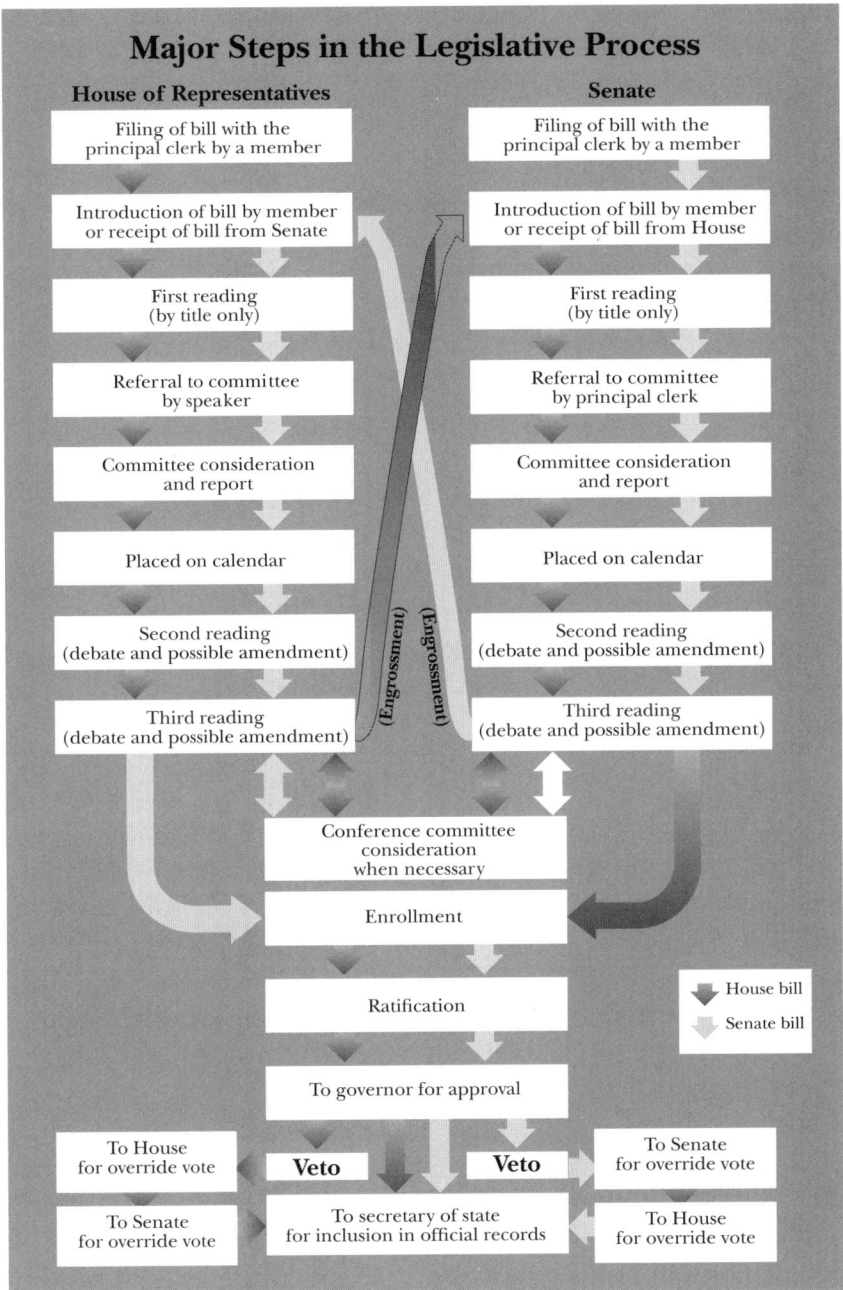

Major Steps in the Legislative Process

House of Representatives

- Filing of bill with the principal clerk by a member
- Introduction of bill by member or receipt of bill from Senate
- First reading (by title only)
- Referral to committee by speaker
- Committee consideration and report
- Placed on calendar
- Second reading (debate and possible amendment)
- Third reading (debate and possible amendment)

Senate

- Filing of bill with the principal clerk by a member
- Introduction of bill by member or receipt of bill from House
- First reading (by title only)
- Referral to committee by principal clerk
- Committee consideration and report
- Placed on calendar
- Second reading (debate and possible amendment)
- Third reading (debate and possible amendment)

(Engrossment)

Conference committee consideration when necessary

Enrollment

Ratification

To governor for approval

House bill

Senate bill

To House for override vote — **Veto** — **Veto** — To Senate for override vote

To Senate for override vote — To secretary of state for inclusion in official records — To House for override vote

Source: Joseph S. Ferrell, *The General Assembly of North Carolina: A Handbook for Legislators*, seventh ed. (Chapel Hill, N.C.: The University of North Carolina at Chapel Hill, Institute of Government, 1997), p. 51.

The deadlines are usually set in the Senate and House rules adopted for that session. There will be several deadlines relatively early in the session for introduction of bills—often separate deadlines for public bills, local bills, and departmental bills (after these deadlines, bills cannot be introduced except by suspension of the rules). Deadlines are also set in both houses in the first regular session for "crossover" of bills—dates by which a bill must pass one house in order to be eligible for consideration in the second regular session.

Early in any first regular session the districts should insist that the North Carolina Department of Environment and Natural Resources (DENR or the Division) supply them with the deadlines for that session, so that the district supervisors will be aware of deadlines they should meet with respect to bills that they sponsor.

8. What requirements should districts be aware of with respect to lobbying legislators?

The North Carolina Lobbying Law requires that any lobbyist file a registration statement with the Secretary of State before engaging in any lobbying. Lobbyists also must meet other requirements such as filing statements of lobbying expenses and they must pay a $200 registration fee. (See G.S. 120-47.2, -47.3, -47.6, and -47.7.)

The definition of "lobbyist" under this law is any individual who (a) is employed and receives compensation, or who contracts for economic consideration, for the purpose of lobbying, or (b) represents another person and receives compensation for the purpose of lobbying. [See G.S. 120-47.1(6).] Individual district supervisors who seek to persuade their legislators to agree with their positions on proposed legislation clearly are not required to register as lobbyists. The chair of the the State Association's Legislative Committee who contacts legislators on behalf of the Association is not required to register as a lobbyist either, as the Division now interprets the statute. Any supervisor who represents the State Association in this capacity should contact the Division early in any legislative session for an opinion on this matter.

9. How do districts and their conservation partners prepare for legislative action?

District supervisors, the State Association of Districts, the Division of Soil and Water Conservation, DENR, and the Governor all have roles to play in preparing for legislative action.

THE STATE ASSOCIATION. Traditionally, the State Association has been a regular vehicle for developing proposals for state legislation and for the state budget. Districts have an opportunity to submit proposals for legislation and other policy proposals at fall area meetings. At the January annual meeting of the State Association these proposals are considered by the State Association's committees, and those that are approved are considered at the meeting of the entire State Association. After the annual meeting, the chair of the State Association's Legislative Committee usually assumes responsibility for presenting the association's legislative program to the General Assembly. In odd-numbered years this involves almost immediate follow-up after the annual meeting, and in even-numbered years a more leisurely follow-up. (See Question 6 in this chapter.)

THE STATE LEVEL. At the state level there are several potential players in the legislative process affecting districts: the secretary of DENR and the Division of Soil and Water Conservation; the State Commission and its chair; the Attorney General's office or Institute of Government for drafting; and the Governor and DENR's legislative liaison officer. The extent to which any of these is involved varies from year to year. Ultimately, someone must contact individual senators and representatives to sponsor budgetary and other legislative proposals in the General Assembly. Sometimes senators and representatives with a record of support for soil and water conservation will play a role in legislative planning and follow-up. The chair of the legislative committee of the State Association will work with the state-level players who are involved in any particular year.

THE DISTRICTS. District supervisors can play an important role in developing legislation and state budget proposals of their own leading up to the fall area meetings. During legislative sessions, district supervisors may be called on to support or oppose legislation and individual district supervisors may also have legislative proposals of their own that they want to pursue with their senators and representatives independent of the proposals that go through the regular area and annual meeting process.

Figure 12.4. The "Who?" "What?" "When?" "Where?" and "How?" of Working with Legislators and County Commissioners

Here is a basic set of questions for district supervisors to ask themselves about their strategy for working with their legislators and county commissioners. They are meant to be food for thought—some questions worth asking by a new supervisor and worth repeating from time to time by experienced supervisors. There are no simple or set answers to some of these questions, because they involve issues of strategy or circumstances that vary from one person or one time to another. These questions fall into five groups.

1. *What* is on your local or state legislative agenda?

2. *Who* should be contacted? Who should make the contacts?

3. *When* do you need proposals ready to fit other people's calendars? In what form?

4. *Where* do you best make your contacts with legislators?

5. *How* do you coordinate?
   With whom?

    Who?
1. Who is the person to contact?
2. Should you try to reach more than one legislator or commissioner?
3. Should you personally try to work *directly* with legislators at all, or would it be better to reach legislators or commissioners indirectly through others?
4. If you decide to approach legislators indirectly, whom should you contact?

   - Personal staff of a legislator or commissioner?
   - Other county staff (such as the county manager) or legislative staff (such as the fiscal research staff)?
   - Departmental spokesmen (for example, in DENR) or the State Soil and Water Conservation Commission?
   - The State Association (through the president or the chair of the Legislative Committee)?
   - A lobbyist?

Who?
(cont'd)

5. Should your object be to reach your individual legislator or commissioner and let them carry the ball from there, or should you try to reach key leaders directly (such as a chairman of a key legislative committee, or the speaker of the House or Lieutenant Governor, or president pro tempore of the Senate, or the chairman of the county commissioners)?

6. From the supervisors' end of things, who should make the contacts: Any supervisor? Only your chairman? Only the elected supervisors?

7. On any given proposal, who are the key people that you really have to persuade to go your way: One legislator or commissioner? Your delegation—that is, all the legislators in your legislative districts? A particular legislative committee?

What?

1. What is on the district's agenda for legislators or county commissioners?

2. If there is more than one item, what are your priorities? How many times can you "go to the well" with these groups this year (this month, or this biennium)?

3. Should you always keep up some minimum legislative contacts, even if you have no particular proposals pending, or should you wait to contact legislators and commissioners until you have something specific to ask for? How early in the development of a proposal should you be in contact with one or more legislators or commissioners?

4. What form should your proposal take—an outline, a narrative, a draft bill, or an ordinance? What kind of technical help do you need in order to get the proposal in this form?

5. What special preparations need to be made for a formal presentation of your proposal?

6. What procedures must be followed to get action by the General Assembly or county commissioners?

7. What legal or customary restrictions are there on the way a supervisor proceeds in dealing with these groups? For example, are there any pertinent restrictions on "lobbying"? Any restrictions on dealing with legislative staff? Any restrictions on how a state conservation official can work on legislative matters?

(continued on page 122)

When?   1. When do you need to get proposals ready in order to fit them
            into the legislative calendar of regular sessions in odd-numbered
            years and special sessions at other times? When are the bill
            introduction deadlines in the Senate and House? When are the
            "crossover dates" in the Senate and House? (The crossover date
            is the date by which a bill must pass one house in order to be
            eligible for consideration in the short legislative session.)
         2. When do you need to get proposals ready in order to fit into
            the agenda of monthly (or more frequent) county commission-
            ers' meetings?
         3. If your proposals need the endorsement of the State Soil and
            Water Commission or the State Association, when do you
            need to prepare a proposal in order to fit into the timing of
            their meetings?

Where?   1. Do you need to go to a formal legislative committee meeting
            or hearing, or county commissioners' meeting? Where will it
            be held?
         2. Where is it best to make your first and subsequent contacts
            with a legislator or commissioner: at his or her home? per-
            sonal office? public office?
         3. What can best be handled by phone or e-mail or in informal
            contacts, and what needs to be handled in person?

Ten Guidelines for Working with Legislators and County Commissioners

Here are ten guidelines to keep in mind when working with legislators
and county commissioners.

ONE. Get to know your legislators and county commissioners early
in your service as a district supervisor. Don't wait until you have to
ask them for something.

TWO. Learn what positions each commissioner and legislator is
likely to take on issues that matter to your district. Develop a strategy
for taking advantage of the "plus factors" and coping with the "minus
factors."

Where?
(cont'd)

4. What are some informal gatherings where you can often do business best with a legislator or commissioner? Where and when do they happen?

How?

In asking how to proceed, supervisors are focusing on questions of strategy and tactics. Some of these questions have already been raised under "Who," "What," "When," and "Where." Here are a few more pertinent How questions:

1. How do you decide whom you should approach on these matters?
2. How do you coordinate with other supervisors and districts? How do you work through the State Association, the State Commission, and the State Division of Soil and Water Conservation?
3. How should supervisors organize to deal with matters where they take the initiative? With defensive matters where they have to react to proposals developed by outsiders?

Go or
not go?

Based on your best judgment and all the good advice you can get, is it really worth trying to get your proposal adopted? Or is the chance of winning too slight or the cost of winning too high to be worth it—at least for the time being?

THREE. Learn to count the votes before you ask something of your board of commissioners or your legislative delegation. Ordinarily, don't ask for something they won't give you.

FOUR. Make the effort to reach your commissioners a team effort, with input from all supervisors and staff. Consider making legislator and commissioner relations a regular district board meeting agenda item.

FIVE. Come to terms as a board with the politics of relationships with legislators and commissioner. If possible, pair up your district supervisors with legislators and commissioners of the same political party, or pair a non-partisan supervisor with a county commissioner who is not politically aligned.

SIX. Be prepared to tell your commissioners and legislators the story of the dollars and other resources that your district, DENR, and NRCS bring to your county. Ask your regional coordinator for help with this story.

SEVEN. Consider field trips to put your district's best foot forward with presentations by your district's best spokespersons—whether staff or supervisors. Invite commissioners and legislators to appear or speak at district board meetings.

EIGHT. Prepare yourself to do a good job for your district when you are getting ready to meet with your commissioners and legislators—be ready to deliver good content in good style.

NINE. Learn the legislative and commissioner calendars and schedules by heart, and fit your schedule to those calendars. Time is of the essence in dealing with legislative bodies. (The calendars include dates when these bodies and their committees meet and deadlines for matters like introduction and passage of bills and other proposals. The schedules of individual legislators and commissioners will tell you when you can expect to talk with them.) Check these calendars and schedules with your regional coordinators and the legislative committee chair for the State Association. Learn what forms of communication suit the legislators and commissioners—personal meeting, conversations, e-mail, voice mail, and so on. Learn what needs to be addressed with staff members rather than individual legislators or commissioners.

TEN. "Stick around" in dealing with legislators and commissioners. Many frustrated suitors have learned the hard way that "it ain't over till it's over." Elected politicians have to deal with constituents with many diverse views. Sometimes the elected politicians may respond to the last voice they hear. If you are not around to remind them of your concerns, if only by being there, they may forget you.

13

Federal Programs of Interest to Districts

Dick Fowler

The Operational Agreement between the U.S. Department of Agriculture Natural Resources Conservation Service (USDA–NRCS), the N.C. Department of Environment and Natural Resources Division of Soil and Water Conservation (DENR and the Division), individual soil and water conservation districts, and their corresponding county governments includes the statement,

> The parties recognize the natural resources conservation program as a unique blend of voluntary conservation initiatives and federal, state, and local mandates. Together these address a variety of natural resource, environmental, and educational issues. The parties agree to jointly commit their program authorities and financial and human resources to cooperatively implement a unified natural resources conservation program in areas of mutual concern. The implementation of all programs will be done in accordance with program policy and procedure developed for that specific program.

NRCS has been charged by Congress to administer a number of federal programs that have a positive impact on local conservation programs. All of these programs provide for technical assistance to land users, and a number of the programs offer cost-share or financial assistance as well. Such programs and financial resources, coupled with those provided by the state and local units of government, provide the technical and financial assistance that is critical for the implementation of a total conservation program.

Dick Fowler is assistant state conservationist for North Carolina's Natural Resources Conservation Service.

A number of the program authorities and financial resources available through NRCS are authorized through the Farm Bill.

1. What exactly is the Farm Bill?
This term is broadly used to describe national legislation that is drafted, debated, and eventually agreed upon by both houses of Congress and signed into law by the president. Typically, there is a new Farm Bill every five to seven years. This legislation greatly impacts the programs and authorities of NRCS and, therefore, can have a significant impact on the conservation partnership. NRCS, as part of the executive branch of federal government, is obligated to follow the language of the Farm Bill and implement the specific programs contained in that legislation.

2. What part of the Farm Bill has the greatest impact on NRCS?
From a broad perspective, there are several primary areas within the Farm Bill, which include commodity programs, conservation, trade, nutrition, rural development, research, forestry, and energy. The conservation title contains the language and program authorities of greatest interest to NRCS and therefore to the overall partnership.

3. Does the Farm Bill mandate priorities for NRCS that conflict with those of the partnership in North Carolina?
In the past, priorities within the Farm Bill have closely mirrored those of the North Carolina partnership, that is, erosion control on cropland, animal agriculture, wetland restoration, forestry, and grazing lands. Agriculture in North Carolina is extremely diverse. Therefore, a serious conflict between priorities within the state and any given Farm Bill is remote, although the possibility for some conflict is always present.

4. Is each Farm Bill similar to the previous one, or can they be significantly different?
Farm Bills can be significantly different and can cause a major shift in farm policy and conservation programs. A clear example was the creation of "Freedom to Farm" language in the 1996 legislation, which did not previously exist and was repealed in the 2002 legislation. Also, conservation programs can change with new Farm Bills, creating new

programs and/or abolishing previous programs. As an example, the 2002 Farm Bill created two new programs entitled the Conservation Security Program and the Private Grazing Lands Initiative.

5. During the recent past, which Farm Bill has had the greatest impact on the partnership?
Although all Farm Bills have been important to the partnership, three specific ones come to mind. The 1985 Farm Bill introduced the concepts of conservation compliance, sodbuster, and swamp buster. NRCS was charged with the responsibility of identifying highly erodible land, determining the adequacy of the conservation treatment on that land, and reporting to the Farm Service Agency (FSA) if a land user was not in compliance with their conservation plan. In addition, the agency was required to notify The Farm Service Agency (FSA) of any violations of the provisions of the sodbuster and/or swamp buster programs. In the minds of many people, these enforcement responsibilities under the 1985 Farm Bill changed the pure "white hat" voluntary approach of NRCS to a tint of gray, implying some regulatory authority. The 1996 Farm Bill created a number of new conservation programs that are still important to the conservation partnership today, namely the Environmental Quality Incentives Program (EQIP), the Wildlife Habitat Incentives Program (WHIP), and the Farm and Ranchland Protection Program. These programs provided cost-share assistance to land users while also providing technical assistance funds to NRCS. The 2002 Farm Bill will be remembered as having the strongest conservation title of any Farm Bill in history. Potential funding for conservation programs was increased approximately 80 percent, and several new programs were added.

6. Why is it important for the conservation partnership to implement Farm Bill programs?
The conservation partnership should work to maximize the use of all available conservation programs, including federal, state, and local programs. In order to maximize the statewide conservation program and have the greatest possible positive impact, all programs must be used to their fullest potential. For example, if NRCS is not successful in implementing its programs, the agency's funding will be cut, thereby reducing the number of staff positions available in local field offices.

Approximately 10 percent of NRCS's technical assistance funding comes from these programs. In addition, by maximizing the use of both federal and state programs, total cost-share dollars available to land users are somewhat stabilized.

A good example is the 2001–2002 fiscal year. With the budget picture rather bleak for the state of North Carolina, cuts in the N.C. Agriculture Cost Share Program resulted in a major reduction of cost-share funds available to land users. Ironically, the 2002 Farm Bill increased cost-share dollars through federal programs by approximately 80 percent. The exact opposite situation was seen in the 1990s. Cost-share funding available through the N.C. Agriculture Cost Share Program overshadowed (in total dollars) funding that was available through federal programs. With the conservation partnership working cooperatively to implement all programs, both federal and state, dollars available to land users are somewhat stabilized during the peaks and valleys of federal and state budget cycles.

7. What programs/authorities does NRCS have in support of local conservation programs?
A number of programs are described briefly below.
CONSERVATION TECHNICAL ASSISTANCE (CTA). NRCS's largest conservation program, Conservation Technical Assistance provides the staff and infrastructure (science and technology, engineering, technical standards, data, and other support) for delivering technical assistance to support all USDA–related conservation programs. The primary purpose of the program is to ensure that all land users, including farmers, homeowners, communities and groups, private businesses, and other units of government, have the sound, science-based technical assistance needed to plan and implement conservation systems. This program provides the technical assistance for individuals to comply with federal, state, and local laws and regulations as well as to apply voluntary conservation. The CTA program also collects, analyzes, interprets, and disseminates information through the National Resources Inventory about the condition and trends of the nation's soil and other natural resources. This program develops and supports field office technical guides, technical references, practice standards, and planning procedures. No cost-share funding is available through the CTA program, but technical assistance is available in all 100 counties of North Carolina.

CONSERVATION RESERVE PROGRAM (CRP) CONTINUOUS SIGN-UP. The purpose of continuous Conservation Reserve Program sign-up is, by focusing on selected practices and landscapes, to provide environmental benefits to large areas relative to the acreage on which the practices are applied. Participants may enroll eligible land in ten- to fifteen-year contracts that specify conservation practice requirements to meet the producer's objectives. This program provides rental payments for enrolled acres based on the agriculture rental value of the land and provides cost-share assistance for up to 50 percent of the participant's costs in establishing approved conservation practices. Examples of conservation practices include riparian buffers, filter strips, grassed waterways, windbreaks, and shallow water areas for wildlife. Additional financial assistance may be available for practice maintenance, and a practice and signing incentive bonus is also available. Land offered for the Conservation Reserve Program must be cropland that was planted to an agricultural commodity two of the last five years or must be marginal pastureland suitable for use as a riparian buffer planted to trees. Continuous CRP sign-up is available in all counties of North Carolina, and offers are automatically accepted, provided the acreage and producer meet certain eligibility requirements. The Farm Service Agency has administrative responsibility for this program with NRCS having technical responsibility.

CONSERVATION RESERVE PROGRAM (CRP) GENERAL SIGN-UP. The Conservation Reserve Program offered during a general sign-up is a voluntary program that offers annual rental payments, incentive payments for certain practices, and cost-share payments to establish conservation cover on highly erodible cropland or marginal pastureland. Offers for CRP contracts are ranked using an environmental benefit index, and those offers having the highest environmental benefit are accepted into the program. Participants accepted into the program enroll eligible land in ten- to fifteen-year contracts, and a conservation plan is developed for each contract. Landowners may only make offers for CRP contracts during specified "sign-up periods." CRP provides rental payments for acres enrolled in the program based on the agriculture rental value of the land and provides cost-share assistance for up to 50 percent of the participant's costs in establishing approved conservation practices. Land offered for CRP must be cropland that was planted to an agricultural commodity two of the last five years.

CONSERVATION RESERVE ENHANCEMENT PROGRAM (CREP). The Conservation Reserve Enhancement Program, an enhancement to regular CRP, is a state–federal conservation partnership program targeted to address significant water quality, soil erosion, and wildlife habitat concerns specific to a state and the nation. The North Carolina CREP includes environmentally sensitive cropland and marginal pastureland within the Chowan, Neuse, and Tar-Pamlico river basins, as well as the Jordan Lake watershed area. Participants may choose to enroll acreage as a ten-year or fifteen-year contract or as thirty-year and permanent conservation easements. Eligible practices include riparian buffers planted to trees, filter strips, wetland restoration, and hardwood tree planting. USDA makes annual rental payments for contracts up to fifteen years and also pays 50 percent of the cost to install the eligible conservation practices. The state of North Carolina will pay a bonus at the time the land is enrolled to participants who enroll acreage in thirty-year contracts or permanent agreements. The state also provides a cost-share payment for installing eligible practices at a rate of 25 to 50 percent, depending upon the length of the agreement. Overall leadership for CREP is provided by the N.C. Division of Soil and Water Conservation and the Farm Service Agency. Technical support is provided by NRCS.

ENVIRONMENTAL QUALITY INCENTIVES PROGRAM (EQIP). One of the better known Farm Bill programs, the Environmental Quality Incentives Program provides technical assistance, cost-share programs, incentive payments, and education to producers to address a broad range of soil, water, air, wildlife, and related natural resource concerns on North Carolina's farms. EQIP is available to producers who enter into multi-year contracts based on conservation plans. This program is locally led with conservation districts identifying specific resource concerns and priorities; providing input on cost-share practices and helping to establish ranking criteria for evaluating applications; and establishing a procedure for approving applications. Applications are selected based on the degree of environmental benefit. EQIP pays up to 75 percent of the costs for installing conservation practices and incentive payments for producers to try new management practices. Many conservation practices in the field office technical guide are eligible for cost sharing through EQIP. Contracts may include cropland, hay land, grazing land, wetlands, wildlife land, or forestland. Applications are accepted year-round; however, each county will identify dates to rank and select applications for funding. Technical assistance is provided through NRCS and local conservation districts. Cost-share funding is provided through the Commodity Credit Corporation and is administered by the Farm Service Agency.

WILDLIFE HABITAT INCENTIVES PROGRAM (WHIP). This program provides technical assistance and cost-share payments to landowners for the restoration, development, and management of wildlife habitats. Producers enter into multi-year Wildlife Habitat Development Agreements. In North Carolina, WHIP prioritizes funding for agreements that help restore, enhance, and properly manage native grasslands, pine savannas, prairie remnants, old-fields, and native vegetation on field borders. This program pays 75 percent of the average cost to install practices included in the Wildlife Habitat Development Agreement. The WHIP is available in all counties, and sign-up is on a continuous basis. Examples of commonly used practices include establishing native plants to enhance wildlife cover and food resources, managing field borders and woodland openings to provide habitat, fencing to exclude livestock from sensitive habitat areas, and prescribed burning to increase plant diversity.

WETLANDS RESERVE PROGRAM (WRP). The WRP is a voluntary program offering landowners the opportunity to protect, restore, and enhance wetlands on their property. WRP offers three options for landowners to participate in the program: permanent easements, thirty-year easements, or ten-year restoration cost-share agreements. In all cases, the landowner retains ownership, access, and responsibility for the land. Under WRP, landowners receive a payment for the easement, as well as cost-share payment for restoring the wetland. Payments are as follows: *permanent easements*—USDA pays 100 percent of the cost to restore the wetland, the legal costs to establish the easement, and a payment for the easement equal to the lesser of a county-based rate cap, the appraised agricultural value, or the amount offered by the landowner; *thirty-year easement*—USDA pays 75 percent of what would be paid for a permanent easement, 100 percent of the legal cost, and 75 percent of the restoration costs; *ten-year restoration cost-share agreement*—USDA pays 75 percent of the cost of restoring degraded wetland and associated upland. The WRP program is administered by NRCS, and applications are accepted year-round.

SOIL SURVEY. NRCS has leadership responsibility for the National Cooperative Soil Survey Program. The primary purpose of this program is the delineation and classification of all the land area in the state by soil type. The State of North Carolina, through the Division of Soil and Water Conservation, is a strong partner in this program, providing field soil scientists to assist with the mapping efforts. In addition, county governments and others contribute funds to the soil survey program. North Carolina will soon reach the milestone of having "once over" mapping completed for the entire state. Survey updates are continuously under way in counties with older surveys.

RESOURCE CONSERVATION AND DEVELOPMENT. This USDA program is led by NRCS and covers approximately 65 percent of the state through ten authorized project areas. The primary focus of this program is community and economic development through grant funding obtained from non–USDA sources. Each of these ten areas is led by a council whose membership is typically made up of conservation district supervisors and individuals representing entities of local county governments, including planning boards and county commissioners. USDA provides a full-time coordinator for each Resource Conservation and Development area as well as part-time clerical staff.

SMALL WATERSHED PROGRAM. This program was authorized through Public Law 566 and provides technical and financial assistance to local units of government to solve localized flooding problems. Works of improvement can include large flood-retarding dams/impoundments and channel improvement. In the future, this program is likely to be directed more toward rehabilitation of existing projects and less toward new projects.

EMERGENCY WATERSHED PROTECTION PROGRAM. This program authorizes NRCS to provide technical and financial assistance following major natural disasters such as hurricanes, tornadoes, flooding caused by unusual storm events, and similar natural disasters. Following hurricanes Fran and Floyd and localized storms in western North Carolina during the mid- to late 1990s, NRCS provided some $28 million in financial assistance to remove debris from clogged water courses and stabilize stream systems. Because of the emergency nature of this program, other statewide conservation program priorities may shift dramatically in order to provide timely staff support to communities affected by natural disasters.

14

Three Basic Agreements
That Support the
Conservation Partnership

Dick Fowler

For over sixty years there has been a strong conservation partnership between local soil and water conservation districts, the state of North Carolina, the U.S. Department of Agriculture (USDA) Natural Resources Conservation Service, and local county governments. This relationship between federal, state, and local governments is unique within governmental circles and is the envy of many agencies at all levels of government. The overall success of the conservation program in North Carolina can be attributed to this unique partnership.

On the surface, the conservation partnership among these units of government seems informal in nature. To the casual eye it is sometimes difficult to distinguish whose employee is providing technical assistance, whose program is providing cost-share assistance, or whose funds are purchasing supplies and equipment. This air of informality and transparency is indicative of a partnership that is strong and working as it should. The fact that this exists in North Carolina is a tribute to the past and present efforts of employees at all three levels of government represented and to the efforts of local soil and water conservation districts and their supervisors.

However, it is important to understand that there is a formal foundation upon which these seemingly informal relationships have been built. Three agreements can be found in every soil and water conservation district office that more formally describe the partnership among the three tiers of participating government—federal, state, and local. Just as the federal and state governments are tiered in their organizational structure,

---

Dick Fowler is assistant state conservationist for North Carolina's Natural Resources Conservation Service.

the three formal agreements have this same tier concept in their structure. It is important to have agreements that include all the tiers of our governmental organizational structure to ensure the broadest possible support for the local soil and water conservation program.

1. *What are the three basic agreements that support the Conservation Partnership?*
The three basic agreements are

- *The Mutual Agreement*, which describes the relationships between the local district, the USDA, and the state of North Carolina
- *The Cooperative Working Agreement*, which documents the areas of common interest of the local district, the N.C. Department of Environment and Natural Resources (DENR), the N.C. Soil and Water Conservation Commission (the Commission), and the USDA Natural Resources Conservation Service (NRCS)
- *The Operational Agreement*, which describes in detail the roles and responsibilities of each local district and its county with the N.C. Division of Soil and Water Conservation and NRCS

THE MUTUAL AGREEMENT. This agreement is the first tier in the series of agreements and describes the relationship between the local soil and water conservation district, the USDA, and the state of North Carolina. Officials signing this agreement include the secretary of agriculture for USDA, the Governor for the state of North Carolina, and the chair of the local soil and water conservation district. As expected, this agreement is broad in scope. The Mutual Agreement establishes the foundation that each cooperating party is independent and has its own respective responsibilities, while establishing the need to coordinate efforts for the successful delivery of conservation programs. Importantly, this agreement establishes that other agreements will be needed to carry out specific projects and activities and encourages the creation of such agreements. The wording of the Mutual Agreement is identical for all conservation districts in the United States.

THE COOPERATIVE WORKING AGREEMENT. This agreement supplements the Mutual Agreement and describes the relationship between the local soil and water conservation district, DENR, the Commission, and NRCS. Officials signing this agreement include the secretary of DENR, the chair of the Commission, the NRCS state conservationist for North Carolina, and the chair of the local soil and water conservation district. Although more specific in nature than the Mutual Agreement, the Cooperative Working Agreement documents those areas of common interest of the federal, state, and local partnership in natural resources conservation. Such areas of common interest include, but are not limited to, sharing of data and information, developing mutual priorities while recognizing individual responsibilities, adopting mutual technical standards, managing staff and personnel, and managing facilities and equipment. The wording for the Cooperative Working Agreement is identical for all conservation districts in North Carolina.

THE OPERATIONAL AGREEMENT. This agreement is the last in the tier of three and describes the relationship between the local soil and water conservation district, NRCS in North Carolina, DENR's Division of Soil and Water Conservation, and local county government. Officials signing this agreement include the NRCS state conservationist for North Carolina; the director of DENR; a representative of local county government, which may be the county manager or the chair of the board of county commissioners; and the chair of the local soil and water conservation district. This agreement supplements the Cooperative Working Agreement and is very specific in nature. It is possibly the most important of the three agreements to the day-to-day operations of the conservation program in a given county.

A comparison of the Cooperative Working Agreement and the Operational Agreement will reveal two documents that are very similar in format and structure yet very different in specificity. As examples, the Operational Agreement is very specific in addressing the roles and responsibilities of the individual parties as related to personnel and fiscal management, purchase and use of equipment/supplies, the development of joint plans of work, and the establishment of program priorities, to mention only a few. Although similar in format and wording, each Operational Agreement is different because each county and each local soil and water conservation district program is unique and different. It is important that the Operational Agreement describe in some detail the specific roles and responsibilities, thereby creating the foundation for a more informal day-to-day partnership.

It is critically important that all district supervisors are familiar with each of the three agreements mentioned above and the specifics of their content. The Soil and Water Conservation District Board, as a group, should formally review each of these agreements at least once a year during a regular board meeting. Office staff should be included in this review as well. The Operational Agreement can be amended at any time with the concurrence of all parties to the agreement.

2. What is the district's role concerning these agreements?
Although local districts will not ordinarily contribute directly to the wording of the mutual and cooperative working agreements, each district can play a significant part in developing its operational agreement. Each district has a special opportunity to use the operational agreement as a vehicle for shaping its conservation partnership with the county and with the district's state and federal conservation partners.

Indexes

Case Index

Subject Index

Abbreviated References

The subject index employs the following abbreviated references that are in common usage among soil and water conservation officials:

DENR. Department of Environment and Natural Resources

district. A North Carolina Soil and Water Conservation District

district supervisors. The board of supervisors (or individual supervisors) of a district.

Division. The North Carolina Division of Soil and Water Conservation.

Foundation. The North Carolina Foundation for Soil and Water Conservation.

Association or State Association. The North Carolina Association of Soil and Water Conservation Districts.

State Commission. The North Carolina Commission for Soil and Water Conservation.

NRCS. The Natural Resources Conservation Service.

A

Agricultural Extension
Services 5, 55
Agricultural Experiment Stations 5
Agricultural Task Force 8
Agriculture Cost Share 14, 43, 45,
48, 51, 52, 63, 103, 105, 128
Agriculture School x

Altria Group Inc. x
area coordinators 8, 58
Association (or State Association)
18, 63, 71, 100
Attorney General 78, 79
audit 27, 35, 39, 40, 52, 81, 82,
86

145

suits against district employees and
 supervisors 20, 101, 102,
 105–109
supervisors (district)
 appointment and election 44, 45,
  55, 88, 106
 powers and duties 5, 12, 20, 22,
  23, 27, 37–40, 42, 44, 45, 55,
  59, 67, 74, 88, 106, 107, 109
 qualifications 19– 21

T

three-legged stool 9, 11

U

Union Mills 5

V

vehicle accidents (lawsuits) 105

W

water conservation 1, 2, 7, 9, 11,
 13, 15, 17, 25, 26, 33–35, 42–44,
 46, 50, 51, 53–58, 74, 87, 113,
 119, 133
water quality management 8, 9, 18,
 32, 42, 103, 130
Wetlands Reserve Program (WRP)
 16
Wildlife Resources Commission
 (N.C.) 30, 49

Index of Proper Names

Individuals

Individuals (*continued*)

Soileau, Daniel x
Sprague, Lynn ix, x
Stevenson, John 96, 97
Summers, Jim 96, 97
Thornburg, Tom x
Truman, Harry 1

Vogel, David ix, 34
Vogt, Jack x
Waters, Wanda 96
Wicker, Warren Jake 112
Williams, Angela x
Younts, Bryce 6, 7, 34

Districts and Counties

Alamance County 97
Albermarle District 6, 12, 20
Anson County 4, 25, 26
Brunswick County 96, 97
Buncombe County 96
Buncombe District 6
Brown Creek District 26
Camden County 6, 12, 20, 26
Catawba County 96
Chatham County 96
Chowan County 6, 12, 20, 26, 96, 97
Currituck County 6, 12, 20, 26
Dare District 91
Davie County 96
Duplin County 63
Duplin District 63, 91
Durham County 96

Guilford County 96, 97
Henderson County 96, 97
Iredell County 96, 97
Lee County 97
McDowell County 95, 96, 97
McDowell District 95
Orange County 96, 97
Pasquotank County 6, 12, 20, 26
Perquimans County 6, 12, 20, 26, 96
Pitt County 97
Robeson County 96
Stokes County 97
Washington County 96
Wayne County 96, 97
Wilkes County 96
Wilson County 96